PRAYERS IN CODE

PRAYERS IN CODE

Books of Hours from Renaissance France

Edited by Martina Bagnoli

With contributions by
Kathryn B. Gerry, Robert Schindler,
and Abigail Quandt

THE WALTERS ART MUSEUM

BALTIMORE

Published by the Walters Art Museum, Baltimore
© 2009 The Trustees of the Walters Art Gallery

This publication accompanies the exhibition
Prayers in Code: Books of Hours from Renaissance France held at the Walters Art Museum, Baltimore, from April 25 to July 19, 2009

ISBN 978-0-911886-72-6

All dimensions are in centimeters; height precedes width unless otherwise indicated.

The Walters Art Museum
600 North Charles Street
Baltimore, Maryland 21201
www.thewalters.org

Library of Congress Cataloging-in-Publication (CIP) Data

Prayers in code : Books of Hours from Renaissance France / edited by Martina Bagnoli ; with contributions by Kathryn B. Gerry, Robert Schindler, and Abigail Quandt.

   p. cm.

"Issued in connection with an exhibition held April 25–July 19, 2009, Walters Art Museum" —T.p. verso.

ISBN 978-0-911886-72-6 (pbk.)

1. Books of hours—France—Exhibitions.
2. Illumination of books and manuscripts, Renaissance—France—Exhibitions. I. Bagnoli, Martina. II. Gerry, Kathryn B. III. Schindler, Robert, 1975- IV. Quandt, Abigail. V. Walters Art Museum (Baltimore, Md.)

   BX2149.3.P73 2009
   242.0944'0747526--dc22

                    2009007812

CONTENTS

FOREWORD

IN THE LATE 1890s, Henry Walters bought his first manuscript, a late fifteenth-century French book of hours, unaware that he was laying the foundation of what would become the largest collection of books of hours outside the Bibliothèque nationale de France. Renowned for its richness and quality, the collection of books of hours at the Walters Art Museum was celebrated in the 1988 exhibition *Time Sanctified: The Book of Hours in Medieval Art and Life*, for the first time calling attention to these consummate works of art as socio-historical documents. The present exhibition, *Prayers in Code, Books of Hours from Renaissance France*, continues the work begun with *Time Sanctified* and explores a group of magnificently illuminated Hours produced in France during the reign of François I (1494–1547). These manuscripts present complex images that challenge received notions of the relationship between the words of the prayers and their illustrations. Shaped around a nucleus of books commissioned by an enigmatic patron, Jean Lallemant the Younger (†1548), the exhibition explores the relationship between the production of printed and manuscript books at a time when evangelical and reform movements were transforming the religious landscape in France.

The aim of this exhibition and its accompanying catalogue is to broaden the discussion of books of hours to include new types of visual narratives emerging in the early sixteenth century, such as emblems books and pictorial Bibles. By looking at changing attitudes toward book illustration, the catalogue provides a tool for decoding the enigmatic images in these painted pages. The manuscripts and printed books brought together in this exhibition showcase a new-found freedom to illustrate the word of God, and they celebrate the intellectual vigor and creativity demonstrated by the invention of new ways to interpret and express the Christian tradition. Eventually, the freedom of invention displayed in these books led to their downfall, as both the Protestant and the Catholic church began exercising a stronger censorship of devotional literature. The books included in this exhibition, therefore, are the last flowering of a popular genre.

In this catalogue, the history of literature, religion, art, and of the individual books themselves is brought to bear on the discussion of the images in these books, continuing a tradition at the Walters Art Museum of providing a firm context for the understanding of works of art, and furthering the museum's mission of bringing art and people together for enjoyment, discovery, and learning.

The production of this volume could not have been carried out without the generous support of a book lover who wishes to remain anonymous. To this friend of the museum I extend the Walters' sincerest gratitude. I hope that *Prayers in Code* provides a measure of satisfaction to him as well as to all those who consult its texts and pictures.

GARY VIKAN
Director

PRAYERS IN CODE

Books of Hours from Renaissance France

MARTINA BAGNOLI

A BOOK OF HOURS is a collection of prayers for lay use, so called because it contained groups of prayers for each one of the eight canonical hours—matins, lauds, prime, terce, sext, nones, vespers, and complines—that, from night until sunset, underscored the rhythm of life in medieval Europe. In its scope and organization, the book of hours was copied from the prayer book of the clergy, the breviary. Like a breviary, the book of hours contained thematic cycles of prayers (offices). The office of the Virgin Mary was of central importance, and it consisted of a combination of psalms, antiphons, and readings dedicated to Mary. Books of hours usually also included the offices of the Holy Spirit, the Cross, and the Dead, as well as the Seven Penitential Psalms. Additional prayers to the Virgin, God, and his saints were added according to the owner's preferences. In addition, books of hours were richly illustrated with images intended to prompt the reader's meditation, thus enhancing the spiritual experience.

Because the text and illustrations could be chosen and arranged according to their owners' spiritual needs, habits of devotion, and taste, books of hours were very personal books. From their emergence in the mid-thirteenth century until the end of the sixteenth century, they were extremely popular.

At the beginning they were the exclusive purview of the aristocracy and the learned ruling class. In the later Middle Ages, with the expansion of wealth and literacy, merchants and members of the guilds also acquired books of hours. Thus, they could appear in large numbers in the extensive libraries of wealthy patrons—the duke of Berry (1340–1416), a great patron of the arts, owned at least fifteen—or as the sole literary possession of a merchant family.

With the advent of printing at the end of the fifteenth century, books of hours were mass-produced and available to a larger number of people. A conservative inventory by the Bibliothèque nationale de France calculates that in the period between 1501 and 1516 an average of twenty to thirty editions of books of hours were published each year in France alone.[1] If one estimates a print run of a thousand for each edition, it becomes readily apparent why in recent times books of hours have been labeled the "best sellers" of the Middle Ages.[2]

Right around the time when the popularity and distribution of books of hours reached their peak, changes in the European religious landscape undermined their position as the prime texts for private devotion. Humanists, Evangelicals, and Reformers sharply criticized the ritualistic nature of Catholic devotion. Advocating a more deeply felt religiosity, Reformers challenged the notion that the performance of good deeds could earn God's forgiveness and argued that God's grace could be garnered through faith alone. The shift was epoch-making, as it affected the manner in which Christians communicated with God.

Until that moment, literacy, and not only the choir screen that physically divided laity and clergy during Mass, prevented medieval Christians from participating directly in the service of God. Only the rare lay person who was fully literate in Latin could hope to achieve an understanding of church doctrine, while others compensated by participating in communal actions measured to identify them as a community of believers in the eyes of God. Most of these actions were physical: fasting, sleep deprivation for long cycles of prayer, self-inflicted pain (flagellants), or displacement (pilgrimages). The ritual recitation of familiar and repetitive prayers integral to the Mass and the divine office in a language they did not fully comprehend was in the same category. Since the beginning of Christianity, oral communal recitation had been an integral part of devotion. The custom originated in antiquity, when the manner of writing without word separation was not conducive to silent reading, but it continued even after the introduction of word separation in the eleventh century made silent reading possible. Oral recitation allowed those who were illiterate or semiliterate in Latin to perform their devotional obligations. Not surprisingly then, Reformers argued that books of hours encouraged "empty devotion," and they cautioned readers to beware "moving their lips without understanding the words of their prayers."[3]

The criticism was not, however, entirely justified. Since the fifteenth century the Church had begun to recognize the importance of silent prayer and encouraged its practice for private observance of the canonical hours.[4] Evidence is found in texts of devotional books, where passages outside those of the divine office began to appear in the vernacular and could thus be read silently and be fully understood.[5] The phenomenon continued to spread, and toward the end of the Middle Ages, books of hours sometimes became, in the words of Paul Saenger, "lay ordinal for contemplation," with vernacular prayers keyed in with rubrics to prayers of the Mass so that the devout could read them silently during the service and would not be excluded from the comprehension of the sacred mysteries recited in Latin by the clergy.[6] A hand-written note in the margin of the June 8, 1503, Thielman Kerver edition of the Hours (no. 5), at the beginning of the suffrages underneath the prayers dedicated to the Son of God, offers a personal interpretation of the Latin prayers: "whether a work day or a holiday, I will always be ready to serve you."[7] These words are made more poignant by their context—the Latin prayer dedicated to Christ the Redeemer and the images of the Last Judgment in the borders. Clearly, the owner of the book promised to serve Christ and at the same time appealed to his power as advocate at the time of Judgment.

In a 1505 edition by Guillaume Anabat and the brothers Hardouyn, the pictures are labeled in French although the text is otherwise Latin (no. 7).[8] A standard representation of the Annunciation, with a full-page image of the Council of Virtues on the opposing verso, decorates the frontispiece to the matins prayers of the Virgin. Beneath the Trinity, personifications of the four Virtues are engaged in conversation. Each Virtue is identified by an attribute: Ecclesia (a church building), Justice (a sword), Charity (a book of hours), and Wisdom (a rose). They are dressed and act like fashionable ladies of the day. Some of their attributes, too, like Charity's book of hours in a precious chemise binding, are those of fashionable ladies ready to go to church (no. 6).

Although the theme of the Council of Virtues originates in the Pseudo-Bonaventure's meditations on the life of Christ, it was popularized in France through mystery plays.[9] Thus its appearance in the Hardouyn edition, coupled with the vernacular language, brings the lofty, doctrinal value of the prayers to a level easily understood by the lay reader. The same association is also exploited in an Adoration of the Shepherds in a 1498 edition of a book of hours printed by Philippe Pigouchet for Simon Vostre and designed by the Master of Anne de Bretagne (no. 3), where the shepherds and their wives are named after the characters of mystery plays.[10]

As the examples above demonstrate, pictures and vernacular language helped mediate the lay person's passage from a semiliterate understanding of scripture, acquired by oral repetition, to a state of fuller understanding that resulted from silently reading vernacular text alongside visual references. It is worth mentioning that Evangelicals and Reformers alike condoned this use of pictures.[11]

This thought is echoed on the title page of a 1533 hours of the Virgin printed in Paris by Yolande Bonhomme, Kerver's widow, which states that the new edition was "recently decorated with new pictures, since the understanding that the letters provide to the learned, images provide to the simpleminded according to the saying: painting is the Bible of the laity; it is indeed through images that those who do not know how to read can read and understand the secret of things."[12] Although allusions to Pope Gregory's remark appear frequently in art of the Middle Ages, the endorsement of the pedagogical use of images seems paradoxical in a book, which after all was made for reading. In light of the shift discussed above and the emphasis on silent reading versus oral recitation, it is clear that in this instance images allowed those unable to read Latin to immerse themselves in the deeper understanding of the prayers. If on the one hand, Bonhomme's remark underscores the Reformers' point about the laity being able to pray only with their lips, on the other, it indicates that images provided a structure that made the oral recitations more meaningful. Praying with your lips while looking at explanatory images made the devotional experience worthwhile.

Since the early Middle Ages, Christians had exploited the didactic power of images, but by the later Middle Ages the invention of printing had made it possible to expand exponentially the number of images on a single page in a book of hours, thus increasing the number of ancillary stories and moral lessons that could be appended. As printing brought books of hours within the means and range of more people, the number of popular images increased. If, two centuries earlier, peasants and animals had frolicked in the borders in topsy-turvy pictures of the aristocracy's estates, at the dawn of the modern era the decorations were drawn from the moralizing lore and folktales of the emerging middle class.

The decoration of the double frontispiece of the office of the Dead in a 1498 book of hours, published by Pigouchet for Vostre (no. 3), has moralizing undertones: it depicts the Last Judgment and, on the opposing recto, the parable of Dives and Lazarus. The pauper Lazarus came to the house of the rich man Dives and was refused a place at his table (Luke 16:19–31). After Lazarus' death, God welcomed him in Paradise, while Dives was confined to the pains of Hell. The pairing of the two biblical episodes forms a stern reminder of the fate of those who do not follow in the ways of God—a message likely common in sermons. In the book, the images in the left border further elaborate this point by including an illustration of the Dance of

Death, a procession of figures from all walks of life toward their encounter with death. Although the Dance of Death first appeared in the frescoes decorating the charnel house of the cemetery of the Holy Innocents in Paris (1424), it was Guy Marchand's publication of the theme in 1485 that made it popular. The dire political and economic situation in Europe following the Hundred Years War (1337–1453) lent even greater relevance to the theatrical *memento mori*.

Famine and pestilence in the late fifteenth century produced anxieties about the end of the world that contemporary commentators exploited. Political events and natural phenomena became signs of the imminence of the Second Coming of Christ. The *Nuremberg Chronicle*, published in 1493, validated Augustine's prophecy and declared the present age to be the sixth and last before the end of the world, while in Florence, Savonarola promoted a violent preparatory campaign of public chastisement to divide the blessed from the damned. It is therefore not surprising to find a widespread use of apocalyptic imagery in the margins of many printed *horae* of this period. Indeed, the advertisement of apocalyptic imagery on the title pages of many editions (nos. 5 and 7) may have had a morbid appeal to the masses.

The most popular motifs appeared in every book printed. To meet the frenetic demand, printers routinely reused woodcuts in multiple editions. A book of hours printed by Dennis Jeannot in 1497 (no. 4) uses the Master of Anne de Bretagne's woodcut of the martyrdom of John the Evangelist, first published in the editions by Antoine Verard and Pigouchet/Vostre. In the latter (no. 3), John sits in a cauldron of boiling oil surrounded by his tormentors. He is serene in the knowledge that his faith will save him from death. The theme of faith is reinforced in the border decorations, which illustrate the theological virtues and the holy sacraments. In Jeannot's edition, the recto opposite the image of Saint John depicts three superimposed scenes of martyrdom difficult to identify precisely. None are specifically related to the text at hand (the Gospel of John) or the main picture. These plates can be traced to a stock in the possession of Verard, from whom Jeannot must have purchased them. The same border appears alongside the terce prayers for the office of the Virgin in a 1498 edition printed by Jean Poitevin, another Parisian printer who was using Verard's stock at this time.[13]

Existing cuts were sometimes chosen for reuse more because of their convenient size than for content. Thus the association between images and text became somewhat haphazard, belying the idea of the images as the *biblia laicorum*. Although it was commercially profitable to produce hundreds of copies of identical books, large print runs ended the personal relationship between the book of hours and its owner, which had been responsible for the success of the genre in the first place. Sometimes, editions printed on parchment would be elaborately colored.[14] Such books were distinguishable from other printed books, but as a rule, personalized books of hours were an exclusive feature of manuscript production.

At this time manuscript workshops, especially in the Low Countries, often streamlined their production and produced hundreds books of hours on speculation. Nonetheless, manuscripts of very high quality aimed at pleasing consummate art patrons and offering a high degree of personalization were still being produced. Since books of hours were outside the control of church authorities, the texts and in particular the pictures could be modified to meet the patron's requirements. Mottos and coats of arms could be displayed in the margins of almost every page (nos. 1, 8, 12), and unique cycles of images could be included. Walters MS w.430 (no. 1) is exemplary from this point of view: the frontispieces for all of the Seven Penitential Psalms show stories of the life of David, from the glory day of his youth through the troubled times of his old age. In the same book of hours, all nine readings of the office of the Dead are introduced by a long series dedicated to Job.

The choice of Job to illustrate the office of the Dead is, in fact, consistent with his value as a type for Christ. Because he was understood to prefigure Christ's Passion, his sufferings were read during the office of the Dead. In late fifteenth-century France, Job's suffering came to symbolize the travails of a population besieged by war and afflicted by famine and plague. His resilient faith against all odds offered a code of behavior that was intended as a model of Christian forbearance. In MS W.430, though, the number of scenes dedicated to Job is unusual. Their liveliness and sense of dramatic action represent a marked departure from the usual run-of-the-mill Job illustrations, and must be related to the personal significance of this biblical figure for the owner.

An even greater degree of personalization is found in a remarkable book of hours made around 1525, now in a private collection (no. 13). Here the images are merely the décor in which the reader is asked to imagine himself or herself. The matins prayers are preceded by the standard Annunciation scene, except that the angel and the Virgin are not there. Before the Gospels readings comes the setting of John's apocalyptic vision, modeled upon Albrecht Dürer's famous example, but John is not there. The office of the Cross is paired with a beautiful, nocturnal scene of the Garden at Gethsemane, but Jesus and the sleeping apostles have disappeared. The lack of *dramatis personae* is puzzling: the main concept governing these pictures is absence. The absence of figures invites the reader of the book to enter the picture as if on a stage—to reenact the sacred stories, while praying. Since the images are envisioned rather than seen with the eye, the reader becomes the artist. These pictures, then, cannot be faulted as part of an "empty ritual," because they depend on the concentration of the faithful for completion. In line with late medieval devotional practice, the images in this book respond to the call for a more deeply felt religiosity launched by Evangelicals and Reformers alike.

Three books of hours commissioned by Jean Lallemant the Younger (nos. 14, 15, 16) also depend upon the reader's ability to complete the picture in the mind's eye. In one, in the Royal Library in The Hague (MS 74 G 38, fig. 5), the beholder becomes a spectator of biblical events as they are witnessed by John the Baptist, who meditates in the immediate foreground.[15] The sacred scenes are so distant as to be almost invisible, and are intended to represent the vision of the saint. A closed book with seven seals identifies Saint John with the actual owner of the book, Jean Lallemant, whose device, a personal coat-of-arms, includes a similar book. Since John the Baptist is Jean (John in

English) Lallement, the scene in the distance is what the book's owner sees in his mind's eye as he prays. His agitation upon contemplating the Crucifixion indicates his psychological and emotional participation in Christ's suffering. As is the case in the manuscript in The Hague, discussed above, the pictures in this book appear only through the mediation of the owner/reader.

A similar strategy is further elaborated in another book commissioned by Jean Lallemant (Walters MS w.451, no. 16).[16] As in the miniature of John the Baptist, the illustrations usually found in books of hours are here relegated to the distant background. The foreground is occupied by a tower labeled *tribulatio* (grievance) that stands on top of a box secured by heavy padlocks. The box is inscribed *spes* (hope) and carries the inscription *hic latet invisum* (here he lies unseen). On top of the tower is an anvil labeled *patientia* (patience) and on it, a plumed helmet and a scroll labeled *probatio* (endurance). From the barred window opening on the flank of the tower, Jean Lallemant, again disguised as John the Baptist, extends his arm toward the sky. There a long scroll unfurls, bearing the words: *mundus veni dubius vixi anxius morior nescio quo vado ens entium misere mei*—a turn of phrase common in epitaphs (I came to the world, I lived dubiously, I shall die, I do not know where I am going, supreme being, take pity on me).

These pictures are not explained by the text of the contiguous prayers, but rather throughout the book, by numerous handwritten annotations that mix prayers and personal grievances. They begin by commemorating the deaths of relatives and proceed to narrate personal misfortunes. Biblical quotes and poetic verse are conflated, to convey a general feeling of unjust accusations. Indeed, Jean Lallement was *recéveur general* (treasurer) of Languedoc for many years, and from 1535 to 1537 he was imprisoned after being wrongly accused of embezzling public funds. In the images in MS w.451 his personal anguish is identified with that of his namesake, John the Baptist (also unjustly accused) and he laments his misfortune as he seeks refuge in his faith. The inscriptions on the base of the tower (*hic latet invisum*) and Jean's scroll (*mundus veni . . . ens entium misere mei*) stress the tomblike quality of the prison.

On the other hand, the tower is decorated with pictorial elements connected with the ideas of hope for the future and resilience in the face of bad fortune. Similarly, an anvil labeled *immerito patior* (I suffer undeservedly) appears in a group of drawings in a manuscript at the Morgan Library in New York (MS M.438).[17] The theme continues in later collections and appears, for example, as a symbol of strength in Theodore Beze's *Icones* (1580).[18] Again, as in the Lallemant book in The Hague, the visions evoked by the prisoner's prayers materialize in the distant sky. We see the visions through his eyes.

In Lallemant's book of hours, each picture is constructed as an emblem, a literary construction that combines a title, picture, and an *argumentum*— a poetic explanation to illustrate a rhetorical concept. As a picture in an emblem, the image of MS W.451 raises more questions than it answers. Its meaning becomes apparent only when it is viewed in conjunction with a text. In this case, the *argumentum* is not that of the prayers but rather the inscriptions labeling the picture and the personal history of the owner, to which references are made throughout the book. In these books of hours, the images are not ancillary to the text in their usual capacity of *biblia laicorum*. Rather, they are integral to understanding the owner's experience of the prayers. The images interpret the text from the very personal point of view of Jean Lallement, and, thus, they represent him.

Lallemant had already experimented with similar ideas in two earlier books of hours where a combination of biblical imagery and heraldic motifs was used to create a backdrop against which the text of the prayer could be perceived. In both of these manuscripts, one at the Walters (MS W.446, no. 15) and another in the Library of Congress (Rosenwald MS 12, no. 14), major text divisions are introduced by either a picture of a hair shirt visible through a torn curtain, or one of a seraph standing before a curtain and holding Lallemant's sealed book, inscribed *delear prius* (I shall perish first). The overarching theme is that of Revelation, commonly symbolized in Christian art and practice by a torn curtain and by the book with seven seals and the seraph, both harking back to apocalyptic imagery. Both curtains are filled with heraldic references to Jean Lallemant, who, as we have seen, borrowed attributes from both his namesakes John the Evangelist (the sealed book) and John the Baptist (the hair shirt) as figurative references to himself. Heraldic elements, such as the scattered letters and the cut knots that are used in other known variations of the owner's device, stress the personal nature of the representation. In the Walters copy, a burst of light in the background contains the biblical scene suitable for each office. Here again, the biblical scenes are presented to the beholder by the owner of the book, whose presence is mediated by his insignia. The opacity of these images is purposeful. The personal narrative of the book's owner/reader serves as the subtext; he is the narrator, and without his intervention there is no solution to the puzzle.

At play here is a personal investment in image creation that reminds one of the words of Marguerite d'Angoulême, who in a letter to her brother, the French king François I, pleaded with him to go with her to his newly decorated gallery at Fontainebleau because, as she put it: "to see your buildings without you is a dead body, and to look at your buildings without hearing your intention about them is like reading Hebrew."[19]

The idea of pictures as word puzzles emerged from the French humanist culture that animated royal circles at the beginning of the sixteenth century. Not only was Jean Lallemant close to the court, but in Bourges, his native city, he made the acquaintance of Geoffroy Tory, a key figure in the evolution of French typography, whom he supported in various publications. In 1529 Tory published a treatise on letter design, the *Champ fleury* (no. 18), where he discussed the allegorical meaning of letters. Tory's treatise was much influenced by the Renaissance understanding of hieroglyphs as ideogrammatic representations of an idea. In Bourges, Lallemant could also have met Andrea Alciati, who was teaching in the city in the period before he published his first edition of the Book of Emblems in 1531.

Alciati's book (no. 24) became an unparalleled success throughout Europe, in part because late medieval visual strategies had created a basis for thinking of text in visual terms.[20] The evidence for this includes illustrated proverb collections (no. 20), mnemonic guides to the Gospels (no. 22), and later, figurative Bibles (no. 23).[21] The development of elusive, personal imagery in French manuscript *horae* of this period should be placed within this broader context.

The books of hours exhibited here demonstrate the last flowering of a popular genre, in which, for more than two centuries, freedom of invention had been virtually unchecked. The source of their success, however, ultimately contributed to the demise of books of hours. As the Protestant church, which abhorred the deeply personal interpretations of prayers fostered by books of hours, gathered momentum, it started to produce standardized commentaries to the Lord's prayers to channel devotion along regulated meditative paths. At the Council of Trent (1545–1563), the Catholic church reacted by increasing censorship of devotional literature. From then on little space would be given to the clever and playful use of words and images that animate the books in this exhibition. After the 1530s, the taste for ingenious and luscious pictures within devotional texts, veritable "prayers in code" designed to titillate the senses and the intellect, would pass out of favor. Soon after, the production of books of hours faltered, and slowly died.

NOTES

1. V. Reinburg, "Books of Hours," in *Sixteenth-Century French Religious Books*, ed. A. Pettigrew, P. Nelles, and P. Conner, 68–82 (London, 2001).

2. R. Wieck, *Time Sanctified: The Book of Hours in Medieval Art and Life*, 27 (New York, 1988).

3. G. Farel, *Le Pater Noster et le Credo en Françoys publié d'après l'exemplaire unique*, ed. F. Higman, 36–37 (Geneva, 1982).

4. For example, Albertus Ferrariis of Piacenza, in his treatise *De Horis*

Canonicus (Rome, 1475). Savonarola also recommends silent private prayers in *Dell'oratione mentale* (Florence, 1492). On this, see P. Saenger, "Books of Hours and the Reading Habits of the Later Middle Ages," in *The Culture of Print*, ed. R. Chartier, 141–73 (Princeton, 1987).

5. Saenger, "Books of Hours."

6. Ibid., 153.

7. "Soyt jour ouuriay ou feste, toujours a vous seruyr ser[a]y prest." Walters 92.82, fol. M v.

8. For early printed *horae*, see I. Nettekoven, H. Tenschert, and C. Zoehl, *Horae B. M.V.- 158 Stundenbuchdrucke der Sammlung Bibermühle 1490–1550*, ed. H. Tenschert and I. Nettekoven. 3 vols. (Bibermühle, 2003).

9. The *Meditations* were a sort of meditation manual written in the thirteenth century by an unknown Franciscan friar for a nun of the order of the Poor Clares and later attributed to Saint Bonaventure (1221–1274). For the popularization of the Council of Virtues at this time and its appearance in manuscript painting, see E. König, *Das Barberini-Stundenbuch für Rouen: Ein Meisterwerk französischer Buchkunst um 1510* (Zurich, 1994).

10. A. W. Pollard, *Early Illustrated Books* (London, 1917), 195. For a discussion of the involvement of the Master of Bretagne (also known as the Master of the Apocalyptic Rose Window) in the design of the prints for the Pigouchet/Vostre editions, see Nettekoven, Tenschert, Zoehl, *Horae B. M.V.*, vol. 1, no. 15; I. Nettekoven, *Der Meister der Apokalypsenrose und die Pariser Buchgraphik um 1500* (Turnhout, 2005).

11. French reformer Jean Gerson, for example, encouraged the use of pictures to bridge the gap between those who could read and those who could only recite prayers: J. Gerson, "Moralité de la Passion," in *Oeuvres*

Complètes, ed. Palémon Glorieux (Paris and New York, 1962), 7:143.

12. "Heures de la vierge à l'usage de Rome, récemment décorées de figures nouvelles, car cette intelligence que les lettres procurent aux doctes, les images l'assurent sans doute aux ignorants et aux simples, selon la sentence répandue: la peinture est l'écriture des laïcs: c'est en effet par elle que ceux qui ne connaissent pas leur lettres peuvent lire et comprendre le secret des choses."

13. Nettekove, Tenschert, Zoehl, *Horae B. M.V.*, vol. 1, no. 6.

14. See essay by Abigail Quandt in this volume.

15. See, on this manuscript and the other commissioned by Lallemant, F. O. Buttner, "Sehen–verstehen–erleben. Besondere Redaktionen Narrativer Ikonographie im Stundengebetbuch," in *Images of Cult and Devotion, Function and Reception of Christian Images in Medieval and Post-Medieval Europe*, ed. S. Kaspersen, 89–148 (Copenhagen, 2004). See the essay by Robert Schindler in this book for fuller bibliography.

16. L. Randall, *Medieval and Renaissance Manuscripts in the Walters Art Gallery, 2: France, 1420–1540* (Baltimore, 1992), part 2: no. 213; Library of Congress, *The Lessing J. Rosenwald Collection. A Catalogue of the Gifts of Lessing J. Rosenwald to the Library of Congress,*

1943–1975 (Washington, 1977), 6 (no. 14); M. Orth, "Two Books of Hours for Jean Lallemant Le Jeune," *Journal of the Walters Art Gallery* 38 (1980), 70–93.

17. W. Voelkle, "Morgan M.359 and the Origin of the 'New Iconography' of the Virtues in the Fifteenth Century," in *Album Amicorum Kenneth C. Lindsay: Essays on Art and Literature*, ed. S. A. Stein and G. D. McKee, 60 (Binghamton, NY, 1990).

18. For Theodore de Beze's use of the anvil as truth, see A. Adams, *Webs of Allusion: French Protestant Emblem Books of the Sixteenth Century*, 129–130 (Geneva, 2003).

19. *Lettres de Marguerite d'Angouleme, Soeur de François I, Reine de Navarre*, ed. F. Genin, 382 (Paris, 1841).

20. On the importance of late medieval visual tradition for the development of emblematic literature in France, see the seminal contribution of Daniel Russell, *Emblematic Structures in Renaissance French Culture* (Toronto, 1995).

21. Ibid., 89–109. On one such proverb book at the Walters Art Museum (MS W.313), see G. Frank and D. Miner, *Proverbes en Rime* (Baltimore, 1937). On pictorial mnemonic guides such as Petrus von Rosenheim's *Rationarum Evangelistarum*, see S. Hindman, "Authors, Artists, and Audiences," in *Pen to Press: Illustrated Manuscripts and Printed Books in the First Century of Printing*, ed. S. Hindman and D. Farquhar, 164–65 (College Park, MD, 1977).

JEAN LALLEMANT'S BOOKS OF HOURS

And French Manuscript Illumination

ROBERT SCHINDLER

G UTENBERG'S INVENTION of the printing press with movable type in the mid-fifteenth century led to the demise of the handwritten, illuminated manuscript, but it was not until the following century that the production of these books significantly waned. The manuscripts made for Jean Lallemant the Younger († 1548) from Bourges, which are the focus of this exhibition, belong to the last great flowering of this art form. At the turn of the sixteenth century, this artistic tradition remained deeply rooted in the mid-fifteenth century, and while it had absorbed foreign artistic trends, the style of painting was still inherently French. When Charles VIII and Louis XII returned to France after their military campaigns against Italy (begun in 1494 and 1499, respectively), among the spoils of war that they brought with them were works of art from the Italian Renaissance. In Paris and elsewhere, local artists quickly assimilated Italian Renaissance forms into their standard repertoires, especially for ornamentation. Printed books likely helped to spread the new, pictorial language (no. 7).

At least since the beginning of the fifteenth century, artists from throughout Europe had sought artistic patronage in France, and in the early sixteenth century, foreign artists continued to arrive. Certainly the most famous was Leonardo da Vinci (1452–1519) who arrived in France at the invitation of

François I in 1516 and died there only a few years later.[1] The illuminator Godefroy Le Batave came to the French court from Antwerp about the same time as Leonardo, and worked almost exclusively for the royal family until 1522/1524. His commissions testify to the court's appreciation for a painting style that synthesized Flemish, Italian, and French elements (fig. 1). Moreover, his illuminations for humanist-inspired texts seem to echo the French interest, in this period, in classical thought and Italian

Fig. 1. Chantilly, Musée Condé, MS 764 (XIV B 39), fol. 3v, detail

culture: he worked in an unusual grisaille or demi-grisaille painting style, and the miniatures in round format that he occasionally produced were reminiscent of ancient coins or medals, evoking antiquity. Godefroy's repertoire of compositions included designs by Raphael (1483–1520), reflecting his knowledge of contemporary Italian art.[2]

For the greater part of the 1520s, however, French royal patronage of the arts was feeble. François I was preoccupied with military campaigns from 1522 on, and imprisoned in Spain in 1525/1526. The court resided mostly in Lyon, far from the artistic centers of Paris and the Loire valley. Also, several of the most distinguished native French illuminators had vanished from the scene—by 1504 Jean Poyer was dead (no. 1), Jean Bourdichon died in 1520 or 1521, and Jean Pichore is last mentioned in 1521 (no. 8).[3]

Yet a distinctive, new, and essentially foreign style of painting, one that resulted in works of exceptional quality, emerged at this moment in illuminated manuscripts. It was characterized by close attention to detail, delicate surface modeling, and realistic representation of the natural environment. Buildings and their materials—marble, brick, or wood—are carefully observed. Landscapes are sun-drenched, sweeping vistas, and distant horizons are bathed in a pale blue haze. Elegant, sometimes bizarre poses animate the figures, which are swathed in extravagant draperies. Intense, brilliant colors dominate the palette. Gold is used in profusion in the elaborate, Italianate architectural frames enclosing the main images; their elegant proportions suggest three-dimensionality and recall frames of altarpieces. Opposing text pages often feature either illusionistic fruit-and-flower borders or Renaissance designs with columns, vases, cornucopias, or floral elements set against a solid-colored background (no. 11). This style can be found in about ten books of secular content and some thirty books that are religious in nature, most of them books of hours datable from the early 1520s until c. 1550.[4]

A familiarity with both Italian and northern European art is found throughout these manuscripts. Some of the manuscripts' miniatures bear traces of compositions by Raphael probably disseminated through Marcantonio Raimondi's prints. The graphic works of Albrecht Dürer (1471–1528) were highly influential. His prints circulated widely in Europe and are emulated or revised in several of the miniatures.[5] The dominant influence, however, is a group of less accessible drawings and panel paintings by the so-called Antwerp mannerists.[6] Not only do the illuminators copy these compositions, they also follow a similar mannerist style. The Bathsheba miniature in a book of hours in the Walters Art Museum (MS W.449, no. 12), for instance, echoes a highly finished drawing today in Vienna: much of the architecture is faithfully reproduced and two groups of women are largely identical (fig. 2). Meanwhile, the figure of Bathsheba is a copy after Dürer's famous Adam and Eve woodcut, executed in 1504. Yet another example is the architectural setting of the Annunciation from the Rosenwald Collection at the Library of Congress (MS 14, no. 11), which copies a panel by Jan de Beer (c. 1475–1528), a

leading Antwerp artist. It is
again repeated, more freely,
in a manuscript today in a
private collection (fig. 3).[7]

Slight but apparent
variations in execution argue
that at least four separate
illuminators were respon-
sible for the illustration of
these manuscripts. All are
anonymous: the Rosenwald
book is eponymous for the
Master of the Rosenwald
Hours; the Master of Jean
de Mauléon takes his name
from Jean de Mauléon,
bishop of Saint-Bertrand de

Fig. 2. Vienna, Albertina, no. 2996

Comminges, whose arms appear in the aforementioned Walters manuscript.
The so-called Doheny Master and the Master of the Getty Epistles have been
identified as artistic personalities from the same workshop. All four artists
collaborated closely, as can be seen in their shared compositions and stylistic affinity.[8] Their firsthand knowledge of Antwerp art indicates that one or
more of these artists came from Antwerp and that they brought with them
a stock of compositions.[9] Antwerp was one of the preeminent exporters of
works of art in the sixteenth century, and artists themselves often followed
the demand.[10]

Among these traveling artists was the painter Noël Bellemare, who was
based in Paris since at least 1515. No surviving illumination can be securely
attributed to him, but a document establishes that he provided the design for
a glass painting in the church of Saint-Germain l'Auxerrois, Paris, dated 1532.
Several other stained glass windows and also panel paintings, in Paris and

Fig. 3. Washington, D.C., private collection, fol. 20v

elsewhere, show the same style, which suggests that Bellemare was involved in their production as well. This style is also much the same as that of the manuscripts. The repetition of the same compositions throughout all of these works further supports the idea that Bellemare or at least someone in his workshop conceived the manuscript illuminations, too.[11] It was not uncommon for sixteenth-century artists to work in different media, and a surviving document from 1536 confirms that Bellemare did in fact receive a commission to paint a calendar on parchment, now lost, for the parliament of Paris.[12]

Bellemare's Antwerp origin certainly provides a convincing explanation for the style and compositions of this group of illuminations, but his exact role remains somewhat obscure. Is he to be identified with one of the four anonymous artists, perhaps the Getty Epistles Master? Or was he the "designing mastermind" behind all the works associated with the workshop—manuscripts, panel paintings, and designs for stained glass alike?[13]

Whatever the shop's organization, the Bellemare group illuminations are closely interrelated and of a discernibly different character than the mainstream of illuminated manuscripts produced in France around this time. Collaborations among the "foreign" Bellemare artists and local illuminators were rare, but significant. A copy of a secular text by the ancient Greek historian Diodorus Siculus with illuminations by the Master of the Getty Epistles, for instance, also includes portrait miniatures by Jean Clouet († 1541), court painter to François I, as well as historiated initials by a French illuminator known as the Master of François de Rohan.[14] Another book of hours in Baltimore includes a calendar illustrated by an artist from the circle of Jean Pichore, while artists from the Bellemare workshop probably executed the main images (MS W.451, no. 16). A manuscript containing the Epistles of Saints Peter and Paul in the Victoria & Albert Museum has two miniatures by another important artist dubbed the Master of Claude of France and four by two different hands from the Bellemare group (fig. 4).[15] In another rare case, compositions of the Bellemare group were copied by an unknown French illuminator, who collaborated with the Master of Jean de Mauléon in a book of hours.[16] This illuminator tried to imitate Mauléon's style but his miniatures remain recognizably different: he prefers distinct outlines and tends toward a slightly summary, simplified rendering of surfaces. Thus, most local artists absorbed the essentially new style of the Bellemare workshop only superficially, or remained immune to it altogether.

In contrast, it seems that the Bellemare workshop emulated certain pictorial solutions common among their French predecessors, albeit very selectively. Architectural borders were generally in vogue since about 1500, but a small group of manuscripts features certain traits that are striking in their resemblance to those of the Bellemare group.[17] The well-balanced, classicizing proportions and decorative details of frames by the Master of Claude of France are in fact sometimes close, though never identical, to those of the Bellemare workshop (fig. 4; see no. 12). A direct link is further corroborated by the type of script: a book of hours in the British Library with miniatures by a close follower of Jean Poyer and the Master of Claude de France is written in a fine italic, closely paralleled in the aforementioned Epistles in the Victoria & Albert Museum and also in one of the books of hours made for Jean Lallemant and probably executed by the Bellemare workshop (no. 15).[18] Naturalistic, *trompe l'œil* flower borders on text pages that face miniatures also seem to derive from French sources. This essentially Flemish type of decoration quickly became dominant in manuscripts throughout Europe. Although these borders were generally less popular among French artists and

Fig. 4. London, Victoria & Albert Museum, MSL/1921/1721, *fol. 1v–2*

their clientele, Jean Bourdichon, first and foremost, used them from around 1500 in a number of important commissions.[19] A characteristically French variant includes flowering, leafy branches depicted with near botanical precision. It also appears in works of the Master of Claude of France, from where it can perhaps be traced to the Bellemare group.[20]

Thus, while border design seems to depend on French predecessors—or may even have been painted at times by local artists—the main images rely, as mentioned, on Antwerp, German, or Italian sources unrelated to manuscript illumination. This seems to indicate that the painter Bellemare (and his workshop), upon arriving in France in the early 1520s and encountering the special predilection for illuminated manuscripts, combined an established mannerist repertoire with local conventions in page layout, script, and border decoration.[21] This combination must have significantly contributed to the workshop's popularity.

The Bellemare group seems to have been favored especially by Jean Lallemant the Younger from Bourges.[22] Jean's father and grandfather had made a fortune in trade and also held lucrative positions in the royal financial administration, which were passed down in the family. In 1510 Jean was elected mayor of Bourges following in the footsteps of his older brother Jean the Elder († 1533), who had held the position before him. Another brother, Guillaume, became canon and archdeacon at Tours. Thus, by the early sixteenth century the Lallemants were an established family with diverse political, mercantile, and intellectual

Fig. 5. The Hague, Koninklijke Bibliotheek, MS 74 G 38, fol. 69, detail

interests that extended well beyond their hometown of Bourges. Using their wealth, they became important patrons of the arts, and their manuscript commissions demonstrate a refined taste for art of the highest quality.[23] Jean the Younger was doubtless the most enigmatic patron of illuminated manuscripts among the family. He began to commission manuscripts only in the 1520s, and concentrated his efforts exclusively on books of hours; at least six from his collection survive.[24] In terms of their decoration they are among the most innovative and unusual prayer books ever produced.

A full-page illustration of Jean's heraldic lion and his arms appears on the opening page of a book of hours today in the Royal Library, The Hague, datable to around 1540. The miniatures were obviously executed by the Bellemare group, reflecting the refined style and also copying motifs. For instance, the opening miniature for the office of the Dead in The Hague shows the same view of a church façade as folio 61 of the aforementioned hours in a Washington private collection.[25] The pictorial program is highly personalized: Jean himself appears in the foreground of each miniature, while the scene appropriate for the respective text is removed to the background, where it appears as if it were Jean's own visionary, religious experience (fig. 5). This repetitive arrangement is an unusual modification of the scheme traditionally deployed in such books.[26]

Two manuscripts commissioned by Jean the Younger in the Walters are as unusual as the book just mentioned. One has fourteen large, primarily non-figurative, emblematic miniatures in which the traditional iconography has been marginalized (MS w.446, no. 15): the respective devotional subjects for each of the text's main divisions are reduced to tiny size, and situated in a radiant sphere of clouds. Prominently placed at the center of the miniature is either a seraph holding a book with seven seals, part of Jean's heraldry, or a hair shirt associated with Jean's namesake, John the Baptist. Otherwise the book follows the format, Italianate humanist script, and careful rendering typical for books of hours from the Bellemare group. Also, its curious, painted skulls in the lower margins of some pages prefigure the use of the same motif in the manuscript in The Hague.[27]

The other Walters manuscript opens with Jean's heraldic lion (MS w.451, no. 16). The devotional scenes in each of the book's six full-page miniatures appear very similar to those of the previously discussed Walters manuscript, but this time they are incorporated in a repetitive landscape with a massive tower in the foreground. Jean the Younger, locked in the prison tower with his hands folded in prayer, looks out of a window upon the respective devotional scene as if it were a divine vision. The imagery presumably reflects Jean's imprisonment between 1535 and 1537 on charges of fraud, from which he was released after agreeing to pay a steep fine. The landscapes are sun-drenched vistas with steep, rocky mountains, caves, and stony bridges, and the architectural details are drawn with great care, again recalling the Bellemare group. The painting technique is noteworthy as it is unique among Jean's manuscripts and extremely rare in books of hours: with a reduced palette of diluted colors it evokes grisaille. A proper grisaille using sepia, pen, and wash also appears in two other books of hours that have been associated with the Bellemare group.[28] There the iconography is more traditional than that in Lallemant's books. However, one also finds less common subjects such as the Lamb offering the book with the seven seals, which brings to mind the apocalyptic book in Jean's complex heraldry (fig. 6, no. 14). The stylistic affinity among these grisaille miniatures, the Bellemare group, and woodcuts for printed books of hours published by the French humanist Geoffroy Tory (c. 1480–1533) has long been noted (no. 19). It may even be that the Bellemare workshop supplied Tory with designs. One is also reminded of Godefroy le Batave, who repeatedly painted in grisaille or demi-grisaille and happens to be the only example of an Antwerp-influenced mannerist style in France before the 1520s. Godefroy's role with regard to the Bellemare group is far from being fully understood, but the demi-grisailles of MS W.451 are likely to be placed within this wider context as well.

Fig. 6. Paris, Bibliothèque nationale, MS lat. 1427, fol. 13, detail

A fourth book of hours in the Rosenwald Collection at the Library of Congress (MS 12, no. 14) is intimately related to MS W.446 in its iconography, which is the basis for forty smaller illustrations. Nevertheless one hesitates to see the same artists at work. For instance, the heraldic lions at the beginning of MS W.451 and of the book in The Hague, respectively, are almost identical except for the background and the coloring of the legs. On the other hand, their counterpart in the Rosenwald manuscript differs in the book and the helmet (among other details) and also in execution. The attribution of these illustrations ultimately remains problematic owing to the reduced decoration of the book, but they were certainly conceived in the same circle.[29]

Apparently, Lallemant's last commission is a book of hours today in Philadelphia, in which he inscribed his name and the date 1544.[30] At least four larger miniatures seem to be missing, reducing the book's present decoration to red and blue seraphs on the margins of text pages, and eleven initials. Whether a member of the Bellemare group executed the missing miniatures remains unclear; the seraphs, which seem to have been a preferred motif for Jean, clearly differ from those in the Rosenwald manuscript (MS 12) and Walters MS W.446.[31]

The manuscript in Philadelphia, dated 1544, is the only securely dated book in the group. A date of c. 1535–1537 for MS W.451 (no. 16) can be deduced on the basis of the prison-tower motif. The book in The Hague is also late, traditionally dated around 1540, although the exact chronology remains uncertain. The Rosenwald manuscript and MS W.446 (nos. 14, 15) are likely the earliest in the group. They correspond in conception and differ only in elaboration and detail. Ms W.446 is in turn linked to MS W.451, since both include traditional iconography placed in bursts of light. The latter book is the first in which Jean himself is depicted, as he witnesses the holy scene. Finally, the book in The Hague shows the traditional subject not in an unearthly sphere as in MS W.451, but set in the background of varying landscapes or interiors. Lallemant appears even more prominently than before, clad in a hair shirt in the foreground of each miniature, emphatically adoring the holy scene. This chronological sequence seems to reflect the development toward an ever more elaborate and personalized imagery in these books.[32] The book in Philadelphia seems to be the latest, but with the miniatures missing it offers little to relate it to the others. Whether it may have once included the most radical solution, and what this might have been, escapes us, unfortunately.

One last manuscript needs to be mentioned in this context, although no arms or emblems indicate Lallemant patronage (no. 13). Certainly produced by the Bellemare group, it once again reuses, on folio 61, the view of a church façade familiar from the hours in The Hague.[33] The iconography is as unusual as in the other manuscripts made for Jean Lallemant, yet thoroughly different, because it is neither emblematic nor personalized for any one patron. Instead each miniature has a fully articulated setting appropriate to the respective traditional scene. But here the protagonists are missing! For instance, the miniature with the Annunciation to the Virgin shows the traditional interior with her bed and prayer stool. But neither Mary nor Gabriel appears, as one would expect (fig. 3). This unprecedented iconography no longer emphasizes the visionary aspect of the representation and the personal imagery so important in the other manuscripts.[34] Whether Jean the Younger in fact also commissioned it is therefore doubtful. But just like his books of hours, it creatively plays with traditional iconography, and its concept is clearly related to them.

Any attempt to elicit the origin of the Lallemant-specific iconography is also somewhat speculative. One is inclined to see the patron and his intellectual circle, as opposed to an illuminator, behind its conception, however.[35] Lallemant's keen interest in current humanist thought, for instance, is amply illustrated by his patronage of Geoffroy Tory at the beginning of the sixteenth century. Tory's scholarly and publishing activity in the 1520s brought him in contact with leading court humanists who worked at the royal library at Blois, where he conducted research for his famous treatise *Champ fleury*, subtitled "The Art and Science of the Proportion of the Attic or Ancient Roman

Letters, According to the Human Body and Face" (no. 18). It is significant that the Bellemare group can be linked to Tory as well as the Blois humanists. As noted earlier, Tory's printed hours from as early as 1525, which is precisely when he worked at Blois, are indebted to the Bellemare workshop. Among their illuminations for secular texts we find works by the humanists François Demoulins, Antoine Macault, Étienne le Blanc, and René Fame. This may not be coincidental. In fact, the Bellemare group enjoyed royal patronage for their secular manuscripts, much as the Antwerp emigrant Godefroy le Batave had for his illustrations of texts by Demoulins (see page 16).[36] Humanist text, with Antwerp-influenced illustrations, appears to be a constant. This seems to indicate that a progressive style with mannerist and Italianate bias was thought to be appropriate for illustrations of humanist-inspired texts—at least among a certain clientele.

The devotional impetus of Jean Lallemant's books of hours is obvious and, in fact, reinforced through their decoration. Yet, the miniatures are highly intellectual as well, and bear on humanist thought, as is evident from their emblematic significance. Jean's choice of artists, besides his evident appreciation of exquisite artistic quality, may have been influenced by the humanist milieu that employed the Bellemare illuminators for secular commissions. The innovative Bellemare style may, in turn, have been perceived to correlate well with the progressive pictorial schemes of these books of hours conceived in this humanist milieu.

Jean's books depart in a significant way from the illustrative tradition for books of hours, and this may explain their singularity. Unlike humanist texts, books of hours had a largely predetermined decorative cycle, and this convention was, with minor alterations, authoritative. Because Jean's books completely break with this tradition, their iconography is unprecedented. At the same time its conception was made possible only by the very cultural milieu in which it had originated. Owing to their highly personalized nature, these images could hardly be adopted by other patrons, effectively preventing any followers.

1. F. Zöllner, *Leonardo da Vinci, 1452–1519: The Complete Paintings* (Cologne, 2004). See also L. Fagnart, "Léonard de Vinci et la France: Pérégrinations des peintures du maître dans la collection royale au XVIᵉ siècle," *Bulletin de l'Association des Historiens de l'Art Italien* 10 (2004), 121–28.

2. On Godefroy, see M. D. Orth, "Progressive Tendencies in French Manuscript Illumination, 1515–1530: Godefroy le Batave and the 1520s Hours Workshop" (Ph. D. diss., Institute of Fine Arts, New York University, 1976); eadem, "Godefroy Le Batave, Illuminator to the French Royal Family, 1516–1526," in J. B. Trapp, ed., *Manuscripts in the Fifty Years after the Invention of Printing* (London, 1983), 50–61.

3. For these artists, see M. Hofmann, *Jean Poyer: Das Gesamtwerk* (Turnhout, 2004); F. Avril and N. Reynaud, *Les manuscrits à peintures en France, 1440–1520*, exh. cat., Bibliothèque nationale (Paris, 1993), 293–305; C. Zöhl, *Jean Pichore: Buchmaler, Graphiker und Verleger in Paris um 1500* (Turnhout, 2004).

4. The most complete list to date of some twenty-five manuscripts and miniatures was published by M. D. Orth, "French Renaissance Manuscripts: The 1520s Hours Workshop and the Master of the Getty Epistles," *J. Paul Getty Museum Journal* 16 (1988), 33–60, esp. 58–59. Since then several additional attributions have been made, which cannot be listed here in full. From the 1530s on, the influence of Italian mannerist artists, who decorated the Fontainebleau residence of François I, is palpable, especially in border design.

5. See G.-M. Leproux, "Un peintre anversois à Paris, sous le règne de François Iᵉʳ: Noel Bellemare," *Cahiers de la Rotonde* 20 (1998), 124–54, esp. 130–32, with previous literature.

6. For detailed comparisons, see M. D. Orth, "Antwerp Mannerist Model Drawings in French Renaissance Books of Hours: A Case Study of the 1520s Hours Workshop," *Journal of the Walters Art Gallery* 47 (1989), 61–90; G.-M. Leproux, "Un peintre anversois"; idem, "La peinture à Paris sous le règne de François Iᵉʳ (Paris, 2001); K. L. Belkin and N. van Hout, ed., *ExtravagAnt! A Forgotten Chapter of Antwerp Painting, 1500–1530*, exh. cat., Koninklijk Museum voor Schone Kunsten (Antwerp, 2005), 145–49.

7. See Orth, "Antwerp Mannerist Model Drawings," 84, 74 fig. 20, with a reproduction of the painting. For the manuscript in private hands, see no. 13 in this catalogue and note 33 below.

8. These individual masters were identified by Orth in "French Renaissance

Manuscripts." She originally dubbed this group the "1520s Hours Workshop," a denomination that has lately been abandoned in favor of "Bellemare group" (see below).

9. See Orth, "Antwerp Mannerist Model Drawings," esp. 86; eadem, "French Renaissance Manuscripts," esp. 44.

10. See F. Vermeylen, "Exporting Art across the Globe: The Antwerp Art Market in the Sixteenth Century," *Nederlands kunsthistorisch Jaarboek* 50 (1999), 13–29, who provides statistical information.

11. See Leproux, "Un peintre anversois à Paris," and idem, *La peinture à Paris*, esp. 111–12, for details and images.

12. See Leproux, "Un peintre anversois à Paris," esp. 142.

13. See Leproux, *La peinture à Paris*, esp. 134–37.

14. Chantilly, Musée Condé, MS 721. For this manuscript see V. Auclair et al., *L'art du manuscrit de la Renaissance en France*, exh. cat., Musée Condé (Paris, 2001), 46–49.

15. London, Victoria & Albert Museum, MSL/1921/1721. Orth, "French Renaissance Manuscripts," esp. 51–53 and figs. 12, 14, 15, with attributions to the Master of Claude of France, the Master of Jean de Mauléon, and the Doheny Master. For the Master of Claude of France, see also Avril and Reynaud, *Les manuscrits à peintures en France*, 319–23.

16. See E. König and H. Tenschert, *Leuchtendes Mittelalter, 6. 44 Manuskripte vom 14. bis zum frühen 17. Jahrhundert aus Frankreich, Flandern, England, Spanien, den Niederlanden, Italien und Deutschland* (Rotthalmünster, 1993–1994), no. 76.

17. See Orth, "Progressive Tendencies in French Manuscript Illumination," 354–56, for the framing systems in the Bellemare group (her 1520s Hours Workshop); see also Orth, "French Renaissance Manuscripts," 43.

18. See M. D. Orth, "Two Books of Hours for Jean Lallement Le Jeune," *Journal of the Walters Art Gallery* 38 (1980), 70–93, esp. 81. The manuscripts are British Library, Add. 35315; Victoria & Albert Museum, MSL/1921/1721 (Epistles); and Walters Art Museum, MS W.446 (no. 15 in the present catalogue) (Lallemant Hours). In the Epistles the italic script appears side-by-side with a roman book hand (Antiqua). Both feature repeatedly in manuscripts by the Bellemare group, but by no means exclusively. In fact it had been used in Parisian books since around 1500. See M. D. Orth, "Zu Schrift und Dekor des Stundenbuchs," in H. Decker-Hauff, ed., *Livre d'heures Maria Stuart: Faksimile-Ausgabe der Handschrift aus dem Besitz des herzoglichen Hauses Württemberg*

(Darmstadt, 1988), 85–91, with a list
of manuscripts on 102–104.

19. Particularly for the so-called *Grandes
Heures d'Anne de Bretagne* of 1503–
1508 (Paris, Bibliothèque nationale,
lat. 9474), see Avril and Reynaud,
Les manuscrits à peintures en France,
297–300. A facsimile by M. Moleiro
Publishers, Barcelona, appeared in
2008. Anne was queen to Charles
VIII and Louis XII and mother of
Claude de France, whose prayer books
give the name to the Master of Claude
de France are already mentioned as
possible mediator of this motif to the
Bellemare group.

20. See Orth, "French Renaissance
Manuscripts," 43 nn. 13, 14; eadem,
"What Goes Around: Borders and
Frames in French Manuscripts,"
Journal of the Walters Art Gallery
54 (1996), 189–201, esp. 193–94. It
should be noted that flower borders
of this type also occur in manuscripts
from the Pichore group and printed
books of hours with woodcuts from
Geoffroy Tory from 1527 on (see no.
19 in this catalogue). In the Bellemare
group, it can be found perhaps most
beautifully in Getty, MS Ludwig I
15. See Orth, "What Goes Around,"
277, for a color illustration, and more
generally on the Getty book, Orth,
"French Renaissance Manuscripts."

21. A book of hours from about 1510–1515
illuminated by the Netherlandish
Master of Charles V (or his circle),
who worked in Brussels or Mechelen,
features a Bathsheba miniature,
which emulates the same drawing in
Vienna mentioned above. But unlike
the Bellemare pattern, it is combined
with border decoration in line with
the Flemish or more specifically
Bruges tradition; repro. H. Tenschert,
*Illumination und Illustration vom
13. bis 16. Jahrhundert, Katalog 20*
(Rotthalmünster, 1987), no. 25.
Manuscripts from this artist often
feature architectural frames vaguely
related to the Bellemare group, but
the exact nature of this relationship
has never been explored. See T. Kren
and S. McKendrick, ed., *Illuminating
the Renaissance: The Triumph of
Flemish Manuscript Painting in Europe*,
exh. cat., J. Paul Getty Museum (Los
Angeles, 2003), 495–502.

22. For biographical information on the
Lallemant family, see G. Thaumas
de la Thaumassière, *Histoire de Berry*
(repr. Marseille, 1976), 3–4: 409–12;
and J.-Y. Ribault, "Notes sur les origi-
nes de la famille Lallemant," *Cahiers
d'Archéologie et d'Histoire du Berry* 29
(1972), 62–64.

23. See L. M. C. Randall, *Medieval
and Renaissance Manuscripts in the
Walters Art Gallery. France, 1420–
1540* (Baltimore, 1992), 2, part 2:
505–6, for family commissions, with
previous bibliography. See also Avril
and Reynaud, *Les manuscrits à peintures*, 346.

24. Five will be discussed below. A sixth book of hours is yet unpublished. It seems to be an earlier book, which Jean the Younger modified (Paris, École Nationale Supérieure des Beaux-Arts, no inv. no.). The decoration is limited to *putti* and Lallement heraldry. The Walters Art Museum kindly made a description in their files available to me. The manuscript will be discussed in Myra Orth's forthcoming book on French manuscript illumination between 1515 and 1575 (Harvey Miller Publishers).

25. The Hague, Royal Library, MS 74 G 38. See Orth, "Two Books of Hours for Jean Lallement Le Jeune," 87, who remarked on the considerable similarities of the manuscript in The Hague to those by the Bellemare group. The same church view also appears in a Pontifical of about fifteen years earlier, illuminated by the Rosenwald Master or perhaps the Master of Jean de Mauléon (Paris, Bibliothèque nationale, lat. 1226, fol. 22v). For the hours in private hands, see no. 13 in this catalogue and note 33 below.

26. See Martina Bagnoli's introduction in this catalogue for a more detailed analysis.

27. For the skulls, see the reproductions in A. S. Korteweg, *Splendour, Gravity & Emotion: French Medieval Manuscripts in Dutch Collections* (Zwolle, 2004), 199 fig. 169; and Randall, *Medieval and Renaissance*

Manuscripts 2, part 2: pl. xxivb. A tentative attribution to the Bellemare group is made in Orth, "Two Books of Hours for Jean Lallement le Jeune," 84.

28. The manuscripts are Paris, Bibliothèque nationale, lat. 1427, and New York, Pierpont Morgan Library, M.1135. For the latter see Sotheby's New York, *The Inventory of H. P. Kraus*, December 4–5, 2003, lot 326. See also Orth, "Progressive Tendencies in French Manuscript Illumination," 392–94.

29. See Orth, "Two Books of Hours for Jean Lallement Le Jeune," 84, with a tentative attribution to the Bellemare group.

30. Free Library, Lewis E 87. For a description and images, see the Free Library's Web site at www.freelibrary.org.

31. They appear also in the book from the École Nationale Supérieure des Beaux-Arts (see note 24 above) and in the decoration of the Lallement city residence in Bourges; see Randall, *Medieval and Renaissance Manuscripts* 2, part 2: esp. 544.

32. According to F. O. Büttner, "Sehen–verstehen–erleben: Besondere Redaktionen narrativer Ikonographie im Stundengebetbuch," in *Images of Cult and Devotion. Function and Reception of Christian Images in Medieval and Post-Medieval Europe*, ed. S. Kaspersen (Copenhagen, 2004),

89–148, esp. 119, 121. Lallemant's illustrations actually depict the perception of a devotional scene rather than this scene alone. He views the Walters book (MS w.446) as the most aesthetically and psychologically demanding of the group, while The Hague MS 74 G 38 and Walters MS w.451 are thought to be (later) variations.

33. Private collection, Washington, no. 13, attributed to the Doheny Master; see Orth, "Antwerp Mannerist Model Drawings," esp. 89 n. 70; Sotheby's London, *Western Manuscripts and Miniatures*, June 21, 1988, lot 115, 146;

and Sotheby's London, *The Jaime Ortiz-Patiño Collection of Important Books and Manuscripts*, April 21, 1998, lot 39. For an illustration of The Hague, MS 74 G 38, fol. 106, see Korteweg, *Splendour, Gravity & Emotion*, 199, fig. 169. The Pontifical is Paris, Bibliothèque nationale, lat. 1226, fol. 22v (see note 25 above).

34. See Büttner, "Sehen–verstehen–erleben," 116–23, 130–35.

35. Orth, "Progressive Tendencies in French Manuscript Illumination," 387, views Jean himself as the source.

36. Ibid., 141–64.

PRINTING ON PARCHMENT

ABIGAIL QUANDT

THE MID-FIFTEENTH CENTURY invention of the printing press with movable type coincided with the rapid development of a hand papermaking industry throughout Europe. For many reasons paper was an ideal support for letterpress printing. The cost of the materials required for its production (linen rags for the pulp and gelatin for the sizing) was relatively low compared with that of parchment. Paper could be made quite rapidly, in large quantities; it was easier to handle during printing than parchment, and effectively received an inked type impression.

Parchment, typically made from the skins of small, domestic animals such as sheep, calves, and goats, was used throughout the Middle Ages for single manuscript books. It was prohibitively expensive for use in entire editions of printed books, however, as the time and cost for its production exceeded those for making paper.[1] Raising livestock in sufficient numbers to meet a regular demand also presented uncertainties. For these and other reasons, early printers chose to produce only a few copies of a book on parchment, and printed the rest of an edition on paper. The parchment copies, which closely resembled the manuscript books, could be sold at a much higher price to those who valued and could afford the luxurious appearance and greater durability of a book produced on animal skin.[2]

The printing press used during the fifteenth and sixteenth centuries was a modified screw press with two moving parts. The thick wooden platen moved up and down by means of a screw and pressed the paper or parchment over an inked form of lead type that was secured to the bed of the press. The carriage assembly held the form and could be moved in and out underneath the platen by means of a simple pulley system. The paper was held in place between a pair of wooden and iron frames (tympan and frisket) hinged to the front of the carriage assembly. Once the type was inked the pressman would lower the paper onto the form. Owing to the small size of the platen only half of the rectangular form could be printed at one time. This meant that the printer could move the form into place, lower the platen to print the first half, and then raise it while moving the second half of the form into position. The platen would be lowered again to print the second half. Once one side of the sheet was printed it would be placed on a table beside the press. The rest of the sheets for the edition would then be printed using the same form and added to the stack. A second form containing the type for the opposite side of the sheet would be clamped to the bed of the press and the printing of the partially finished sheets would be completed.[3] After the sheets were printed on both sides they would be draped over lines of cord strung just below the ceiling of the workshop, and left to dry.

In order to achieve a rich, black type impression, paper and parchment both had to be dampened before printing, and each required a different process. For an edition printed on paper, the pressman, working in batches of about 250 sheets (the approximate size of a ream), would draw each sheet through a pan of water and then stack the sheets on a board, leaving them overnight under a heavy weight. By the following day the paper would be evenly damp and ready for printing. Although the pressman had to work quickly to print two forms on each side before the sheet of paper dried out completely, the degree of difficulty in working with parchment was greater.

Parchment cannot be dipped in water as it will completely lose its sheet-like structure. If it is humidified the moisture must be limited and slowly introduced so as not to create any distortion in the skin. Although no early accounts of techniques of printing on parchment are known,[4] I imagine that the sheets were interleaved with damp cloths and left under a weight overnight. Once the humidified skin is exposed to the air it quickly begins to dry and curl, so care had to be taken to keep partially printed sheets under light pressure while the rest were being printed. To ensure proper registration of the type on both sides, it was important to finish printing the second form as quickly as possible.[5] The finished sheets of parchment were probably not suspended from cords on the ceiling to air dry, but were more likely dried under a weighted board, to keep them flat and control undulations in the skin. Depending on the area of the animal skin from which the sheet was cut, dramatic shrinkage might occur during or immediately after the printing process.[6] In a book of hours printed by Germain Hardouyn in 1524 (no. 21), the printing at the top of folio Bvii is fine, but the bottom half is difficult to read, owing to the distortions in this area.

Another problem that printers faced when printing on parchment was the difference in the way the hair side and the flesh side received the ink. The flayed animal skin, after soaking in a bath of lime for several weeks, is draped over a wooden beam and the bulk of the hair and flesh is removed using a semi-lunar knife with a dull blade. The skin is then tensioned with cords on a wooden frame and left to dry until it is taut. The parchment maker would scrape both sides to remove residual hair and flesh and to even out the surface. To obtain the creamy white appearance preferred for the production of both manuscripts and printed books, the remains of dark hairs in the follicles had to be removed by scraping away fine layers of skin on the hair side.[7] Despite further finishing and smoothing with pumice stone, the hair side would always have a rougher and more napped surface than the flesh side, and this greatly affected its ability to take an inked impression. Among the Walters collection of printed books on parchment, the ink on the hair side tends to look quite dry and is often much lighter in tone than the ink on the flesh side, which is evenly distributed and a rich black color.

It was hard to avoid imperfections in the animal skins used for making parchment, which presented a far greater problem for printers than for the scribes and artists who produced manuscript books. In the case of manuscripts, each of which was unique, the scribe could sometimes cut the sheet out of the skin such that the imperfection, if very large, ended up in a blank margin. Smaller defects would be skipped over by the scribe, or in some cases would be embellished with decorative scribbles. When used as a printing support, the parchment had to have considerable pressure from the platen to get a good impression. A lumpy area of scar tissue, or an original parchment maker's repair that had been sewn up with thread, could prevent the type from printing evenly and would mar the overall appearance of the page. With repeated handling, and pressure exerted on the sheets from the printing process, weak areas of skin could burst, especially if located at the edge of the block of type. This is seen on a leaf from a book of hours printed in 1497 by Jeannot, where the naturally thin area of a vein has split through (no. 4).

The blocks for woodcuts, metal cuts, or engravings were set up in the form with the type and at the same height (type high) to get the best possible impression. Woodcuts were generally produced on blocks of the right thickness to be type high, while relief-cut or engraved metal plates executed on thin copper or lead sheets would have to be mounted on wooden blocks for printing. The exhibited books are illustrated with both woodcuts and metal cuts. Those printed on parchment seem to suffer the same problems evident in the type, where the inked impression is often much lighter in color and drier-looking on the hair side than the flesh side of the skin. It has been said that the somewhat abrasive nature of parchment could wear down the more delicate surface of a soft metal plate and render it unusable after a certain number of printings.[8] Although this might be the case with the metal cuts used during the fifteenth and sixteenth centuries for the production of books of hours, the number of copies produced on parchment was likely small enough that the opportunity for wear was extremely minimal.

While the trouble and expense of printing on parchment was considerable, the final appearance of these books was impressive. Once the professional scribes had added ruling lines and initials, and the illustrations sometimes colored in or fully painted by artists, these printed books took on the appearance of illuminated manuscripts in almost all respects. Their owners were not deceived into believing them to be unique copies; instead, they were viewed as deluxe and long-lasting copies that rivaled the appearance of books entirely written and decorated by hand.[9]

NOTES

1. While a single copy of a folio-size manuscript might require as many as 150 full skins (one skin per bifolio) a printed edition of 250 copies of the same size book might require more than ten thousand skins—a quantity that would be unlikely to be available.

2. "Special issues on vellum were especially characteristic of fifteenth- and early-sixteenth-century printing, when they usually cost about three times as much as the ordinary copies on paper. . . ." P. Gaskell, *A New Introduction to Bibliography* (Oxford, 1972), 136.

3. The two forms printed in succession were referred to as the inner form and the outer form. For a folio-size book, two pages of type would be assembled on each form. In the simplest arrangement the outer form would have pages one and four, while the inner form would have pages two and three. Once the sheet was printed on both sides it would be folded in half across the longer side. The text would therefore proceed from page one to page four of the bifolio.

4. A detailed nineteenth-century account of the process of printing on parchment is given by William H.

Bowden, who printed most of the editions of William Morris for the Kelmscott Press. See W. S. Peterson, *A Bibliography of the Kelmscott Press* (Oxford, 1984), xxiv–xxv.

5. Early printers experimented with printing with colors such as red, although this required special inking of the type or the setting up of more than one form for two impressions per side. Owing to the extra time involved in color printing, this would have been especially challenging with parchment, where prolonged exposure of the dampened sheet could lead to severe cockling and resulting loss of registration. See Gaskell, *A New Introduction*, 137–38.

6. An animal skin varies considerably in its thickness and the orientation of the fibers from its center to the four corners (where the legs had been). If a sheet of parchment includes a portion of the outer edge of skin this area will be more reactive and prone to distortion.

7. It was only the dark hairs that caused problems, as the remains of any white hairs would blend in with the natural color of the skin and would not

be apparent in the finished sheet of parchment.

8. A technique of steel-facing the metal plates was developed in the mid-1850s as a way to deal with the problem of the soft plate surface being worn down during printing on parchment. See P. Jenkins, "Printing on

Parchment or Vellum," *The Paper Conservator* 16 (1992), 36.

9. See M. Smith, "The Design Relationship between the Manuscript and the Incunable," in *A Millennium of the Book: Production, Design & Illustration in Manuscript & Print 900–1900* ([Delaware], 1994), 23–44.

CATALOGUE

1 BOOK OF HOURS FOR THE USE OF ROME

Attributed to Jean Poyer (active c. 1480–c. 1500), *Death*
France (Loire region, Tours?), c. 1500
Ink, paint, and gold on parchment, 11.4 × 7.2 cm
Walters Art Museum, MS W.430, fol. 114r

The miniatures in this book of hours have been attributed to Jean Poyer, a prominent book illuminator working in Tours in the later fifteenth century, and his workshop. The motto of the first owner of this book, *Ie lay de veu* (I have it in sight), is prominently featured on every illustrated page, and Mara Hofmann has connected this motto to the Le Jay family (M. Hofmann, *Jean Poyer: Das Gesamtwerk* [Turnhout, 2004], 81–83). This miniature opens the office of the Dead, a series of prayers found in many books of hours. Illuminations accompanying this text often depict funeral scenes or personifications of Death. Here Death is personified as a skeleton, a common tradition in late medieval art. His position on the back of a large bull might be related to Petrarch's *Trionfi* (Triumphs), in which the narrator envisions a series of pageants or processions where one concept conquers another: Chastity triumphs over Love, Death over Chastity, and Fame over Death. Illustrated editions of the *Trionfi* were popular in the late fifteenth and early sixteenth century, and provided inspiration to artisans working in a number of media, including stained glass, tapestry, and ivory carving. In book illustrations, the Triumph of Death was often accompanied by a picture of Death riding on a cart drawn by buffaloes or bulls. Although here Death does not ride in a cart, but is mounted on the bull, an educated viewer in the early sixteenth century would likely have recognized a relationship to Petrarch's work. In late fifteenth and early sixteenth centuries scenes of Job increasingly appeared in books of hours (see nos. 2, 11), and in this example a series of minatures depicting the story of Job is dispersed throughout the office of the Dead.

KBG

Sicut quom
am exaudiet
dñs vocem

2 BOOK OF HOURS FOR THE USE OF SAINTES

Jean Poyer (active c. 1480–c. 1500)
and workshop (?), *Job*
France (Tours?), late 15th century
Ink, paint, and gold on parchment, 33 × 22.3 cm
Walters Art Museum, MS w.295, fol. 42v

This book is unusual in that its main text follows the liturgical customs, or "use," of the diocese of Saintes, on the Atlantic coast of France. Very few books of hours adhere to the use of Saintes, as it is much more common to find examples that follow the uses of influential dioceses or major urban centers, such as Rome, Paris, Bourges, or Sarum (Salisbury, England). Its large size is also unusual and could indicate that this book was not intended for private devotional use. Roger Wieck posited that Jean Poyer used this manuscript for training his assistants, and he identified Poyer's hand in small, isolated portions of several miniatures in which the greater part was completed by less accomplished painters (R. Wieck, W. Voelkle, and K. M. Hearne, *The Hours of Henry VIII, a Renaissance Masterpiece by Jean Poyet* [New York, 2000], 40, 41). Mara Hofmann, however, identified two painters at work in this manuscript and attributed the miniature of Job on the Dungheap, which illustrates the office of the Dead, to Poyer alone (M. Hofmann, *Jean Poyer: Das Gesamtwerk* [Turnhout, 2004], 79, 80).

KBG

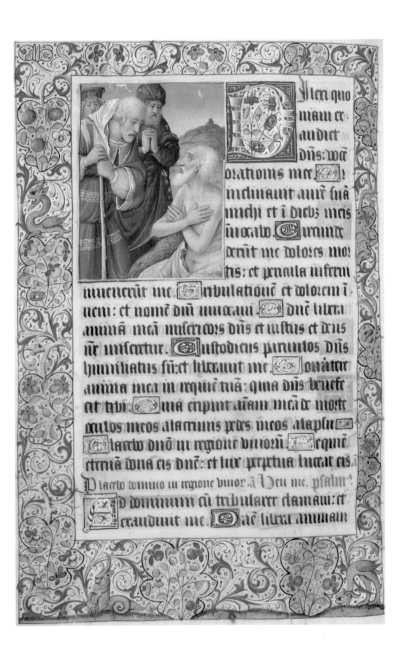

Ilexi quo
niam ex
audiet
dūs vo
orationis mee ꝫ
inclinauit aurē suā
michi et ī diebꝫ meis
inuocabo Circunde
derūt me dolores moꝛ
tis: et ꝑicula inferni
inuenerūt me Tribulationē et dolorem in
ueni: et nomē dūi inuocaui Dūe libera
animā mea misericoꝛs dūs et iustus et deus
nr̄ miseretur Custodiens paruulos Dūs
humiliatus sū et liberauit me Conuertere
anima mea in requie tuā: quia dūs benefe
cit tibi Quia eripuit aīam meā de morte
oculos meos a lacrimis pedes meos a lapsu
Placebo dūo in regione uiuoꝝ Requiem
eternā dona eis dūe: et lux perpetua luceat eis.
Placebo domino in regione uiuoꝝ. ā. Dilexi me. psalm.
Ad dominum cū tribularer clamaui: et
exaudiuit me Dūe libera animam

3 BOOK OF HOURS FOR THE USE OF ROME

Master of Anne de Bretagne, *The Martyrdom of Saint John the Evangelist*
Printed by Philippe Pigouchet for Simon Vostre, Paris, August 22, 1498
Metalcut on parchment, 23 × 15 cm
Walters Art Museum, 91.613, fol. Avi r

Simon Vostre (active 1486–1521) was the preeminent publisher of books of hours in Paris at the end of the fifteenth century. His success was partly owed to his productive association with the printer Philippe Pigouchet (active 1483–1515) and the Master of Anne de Bretagne, the artist who designed the metalcuts. The master sold his designs also to Antoine Verard (active 1485–1513), another influential Parisian publisher of this period, and for this reason his plates came to dominate books of hours printed in Paris between 1495 and 1505. The Master of Anne de Bretagne's cuts are rich in textural details, and he is credited with introducing the dotlike (*criblé*) background that creates a shimmering effect over the white parchment. This page introduces the Gospel readings with an image of the failed martyrdom of John the Evangelist, who was condemned to die in a vat of boiling oil but emerged unscathed. The composition teems with people moving around John the Evangelist as he calmly sits in a cauldron. The saint ignores the frenetic activities of his torturers, confident that his faith in God will spare him all suffering. Beginning on this page and continuing for several others, the scenes in the borders underscore the theme of faith. Personifications of the cardinal virtues Faith and Hope appear on the left and illustrations of the sacraments of baptism and first communion at the bottom.

MB

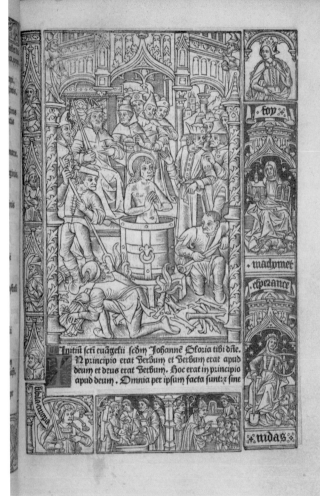

Initiũ sctĩ euãgelii secũ Johannẽ Gloria tibi dñe.
N principio erat Verbum et Verbum erat apud
deum et deus erat Verbum. Hoc erat in principio
apud deum . Omnia per ipsum facta sunt: ⁊ sine

4 BOOK OF HOURS FOR THE USE OF ROME

Master of Anne de Bretagne, *The Martyrdom of Saint John the Evangelist*
Printed by Étienne Jeannot, Paris, August 21, 1497
Painted woodcut on parchment, 17.5 × 11 cm
Walters Art Museum, 91.612, fol. 16v

Smaller printers often reused, and sometimes altered, previously published cuts. This is also the case of Étienne Jeannot (active 1495–1498), who availed himself of plates that had been previously used by different publishers. For example, the Master of Anne de Bretagne designed this plate of the martyrdom of Saint John the Evangelist for Simon Vostre (see no. 3). In this edition, printed by Jeannot, a thick layer of coloring, crudely executed, covers the original woodcut. The colors are dull and many details are obscured: for example, the cityscape visible through the open windows is covered by blue paint, while a man wearing a pointed hat to the left of the Roman emperor is obliterated. Whoever was in charge of coloring must have found the narrative details of the original print overwhelming and decided to simplify the composition. The marginal scenes in the opposite verso come from Antoine's Verard's stock of images and were later used also by Thielman Kerver (see no. 5). They are generic images of martyrdom.

MB

Initium fancti euangelii fecundum Johannem.
Gloria tibi domine.

5 BOOK OF HOURS FOR THE USE OF ROME

Master of Anne de Bretagne,
  The Immaculate Conception
Printed by Thielman Kerver for Gillet Remacle
  Paris, June 8, 1503
Metalcut on parchment, 18 × 12 cm
Walters Art Museum, 92.81, fol. Mv r

In this edition Thielman Kerver (active 1497–1522) adopted with some modification the series of metalcuts designed by the Master of Anne de Bretagne between 1498 and 1500. Starting in 1502, Kerver added some new images to the series, like this emblematic one of the Immaculate Conception. Here Mary is identified as the Sunamite maiden of the Canticle of Canticles by the scroll unfurling above her. She is surrounded by pictures that symbolize her metaphorical attributes, taken from various texts of the office of the Virgin Mary, including the litanies, the biblical Book of Ecclesiastes, and prayers in her honor. Here she is associated with the city of God, the well of life, the spotless mirror, the olive tree, the tower of David, the lily, the star of the sea, the sun and the moon, the rose without thorns, the cedar tree, the gates of paradise, the root of Jesse, the water of life, and the enclosed garden. The picture summarizes Mary's nature as having been born without sin by Immaculate Conception. Although the belief of the Immaculate Conception of Mary had been current since early Christianity, the feast of the Immaculate Conception and its office had been officially accepted only in 1476 by Pope Sixtus IV (1414–1484), when images of Mary and her attributes began frequently to appear.

MB

tota pulcra es ... est in te

amica mea et macula non

electa vt sol

stella maris

pulcra vt luna

porta cli

cedrus

Plantacio roſe

ſine macula

aquariũ viuentiũ

ortus concluſus · ciuitas · dei · fons ortorum

Ad matutinas de conceptione beatiſſime
dei genitricis Virginis marie.

q.i.

6 BOOK OF HOURS FOR THE USE OF ROME

Chemise Binding
France (Paris?), c. 1500
Velvet over beech wood boards including chemise, 42.2 × 29.2
Walters Art Museum, MS w.294

Most books that survive from the Middle Ages have been rebound, either owing to damage to the original binding or because a new owner wanted a binding that would suit his or her own tastes and interests. This book, however, retains its first binding and offers a rare glimpse of the original state of some late medieval manuscripts. Many of the books of hours owned by wealthy members of the laity were bound, like this one, in sumptuous textiles. The velvet fits over the wooden boards of the binding, and extends beyond them to wrap around and protect the book. Bindings of this type, with extended flaps, are called 'chemise' bindings, because the cloth acts as a sort of garment for the book; they are sometimes also referred to as 'wrapper' or 'lappen' bindings. This style of binding, probably adapted from earlier monastic practices, was particularly popular with the laity between c. 1450 and c. 1550. Although few medieval chemise bindings survive, they are depicted in many late medieval paintings, stained glass windows, tapestries, and sculpture, where they are often associated with especially pious individuals (see no. 7).

KBG

7 BOOK OF HOURS
FOR THE USE OF ROME

Jean Pichore (active 1501–1521), *The Annunciation with Personification of the Virtues*
Printed by Guillaume Anabat for Gilles and Germain Hardouyn, Paris, after 1505
Illuminated by the Gotha Master (?)
Painted metalcut on parchment, 22 × 13 cm
Walters Art Museum, 91.614, fols. Bviii v–C

A double frontispiece introduces the matins prayers of the office of the Virgin in this luxurious edition, with the council of the Virtues at the left and an Annunciation on the right. The Virtues, labeled in French at the bottom of the page, are Eglise (the Church), Justice (Justice), Misericorde (Charity), and Sapience (Wisdom). The brothers Gilles and Germain Hardouyn (active 1455–after 1519; and 1500–1541) dominated Parisian production of sixteenth-century books of hours the same way that Simon Vostre and Thielman Kerver had reigned over the preceding century. For this edition, the Hardouyn brothers also used designs by Jean Pichore, a leading figure in French book production at this time (C. Zöhl, *Jean Pichore: Buchmaler, Graphiker und Verleger in Paris um 1500* [Turnhout, 2004]). Pichore worked as a book illuminator, print designer, and publisher. This double frontispiece is closely modeled after Pichore's decoration of a book of hours in the Vatican Library (Vat. Barb. Lat 487, fols. 23–24). With compositions steeped in Renaissance culture, Pichore brings to the printed page the artistic innovations of Martin Shongauer (c. 1435/1450–1491) and Albrecht Dürer (1471–1528), framing his scenes in elegant *all'antica* borders. Although Germain Hardouyn sometimes illuminated his own editions, the refined coloring of this edition is close to the work of the Gotha Master. The feathery touches of gold to the drapery and the thin layers of shadows highlighting architectonic details are characteristic of his style.

MB

Eglile Misericorde
Justice Sapience

La salutation angelicque que baige
du ciel apporta en disant Aue. m. 18
ria gratia plena dominus tecum.

8 DEVOTIONAL TEXTS FROM A BOOK OF HOURS FOR THE USE OF BOURGES

Attributed to Jean Pichore (active 1501–1521), *Crucifixion*
France (Bourges?), early 16th century
Ink, paint, and gold on parchment, 21.1 × 12.9
Walters Art Museum, MS w.459, fol. 1r

This is a fragment of a book of hours that has been split into several pieces; other portions are in London (British Library, Additional MS 39641) and in private collections. The Baltimore fragment contains several devotional texts, including a series of prayers to the Virgin, which opens with this Crucifixion. Rather than depict the historical event of Christ's death, this miniature shows Christ and the Virgin isolated in a landscape, emphasizing the Virgin's devotion to her son. The relatively small scale of Christ and the cross could suggest to the viewer that the Virgin, kneeling in prayer before a crucifix, is a model of pious behavior. The heraldic shield of Jean Lallemant the Elder († 1533), the owner of this manuscript, appears in the lower frame, surrounded by a gold wreath. The book was made shortly after his appointment as mayor of Bourges in 1500, perhaps to celebrate or commemorate that event. Jean the Elder was a member of the elite order of the Chevaliers de Notre-Dame de la Table Ronde at Bourges, and several details in the book, including the shape of the armorial shield in the lower border, refer to this group. The tree branches surrounding the miniature are unusual and might also have been a personal choice by the owner. Elements associated with Italian art, such as the gold Renaissance frame and the *putti*, are found in many French books of hours from this period.

KBG

9 BOOK OF HOURS FOR THE USE OF ROME

Attributed to Jean Pichore (active 1501–1521), *Passion of Christ*
France (Tours?), c. 1520
Ink, paint, and gold on parchment, 18 × 11.3
Walters Art Museum, MS W.452, fols. 13r, 14v

This manuscript was made for Florimond I Robertet (c. 1457–1527), royal treasurer under François I (b. 1494, r. 1515–1547) at the time this book was made. Twelve scenes of the Passion of Christ are displayed in three full-page miniatures, each divided into four parts. The opening illustrated here shows eight scenes in two illuminations: on the left, Christ praying in Gethsemane while the disciples sleep, the betrayal of Christ by Judas, Christ before Pilate, and Christ crowned with thorns. On the right are the Flagellation and Mocking of Christ, Christ carrying the Cross, and the Crucifixion. This arrangement, with four scenes presented in one miniature, was sometimes used for portraits of the four Evangelists in books of hours made in Rouen but was rarely used for narrative cycles. The content and design of these Passion scenes are based on a series of woodcuts of the Passion cycle issued by Albrecht Dürer in 1511. A Passion cycle in an earlier book of hours made for Queen Claude of France (1499–1524) was also modeled on this series of prints, and Robertet may well have seen the young queen's book and used it, or copies of the woodcuts themselves, as a model for his own book of hours. The miniatures in Robertet's book have been attributed to Jean Pichore, who designed illustrations for manuscripts and printed books, and whose clients included Cardinal Georges d'Amboise (c. 1460–1510), archbishop of Rouen, and Louise of Savoy (1476–1531), mother of the king.

KBG

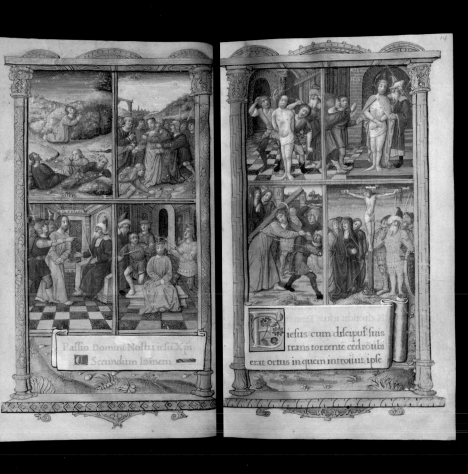

Passio Domini Nostri iesu Xpi
Secundum Iohanem

iesus cum discipulis suis
trans torrente cedron ubi
erat ortus in quem introiuit ipse

10 THE MONTH OF JANUARY

After Jean Pichore (active 1501–1521), *Book of Hours for the Use of Rome*
Printed by Jean Petit for Guillaume Godard, Paris, 1530
Painted metalcut (?) on parchment, 17.5 × 11 cm
Walters Art Museum, 92.83, fol. Aii v

The twelve months of the year are associated with the six ages of man in this calendar cycle. Accordingly, the "young" month of January is illustrated with children playing. The composition is modeled upon one that Jean Pichore had used earlier: in a book of hours for Philippe de Clermont (Morgan Library & Museum, MS 813) and again in 1509, in an edition printed by Jean Barbier (active 1496–1515) and Guillaume le Rouge (active 1489–1517) as part of a richly decorated series with new iconography for many of the offices. Pichore's cycle for Le Rouge was copied by other publishers, including Thielman Kerver. In this 1530 edition, Jean Petit (active 1492–1530) and Guillaume Godard (active 1510–1539), further elaborated Kerver's adaptations of Pichore's original designs. To moderate the differences with manuscript production, paint is applied thickly to the printed page and all but completely masks the print.

MB

IANVIER.

Les sij pmiers ans que bit lhomme au mõde
Nous comparons a Januier droictement
Car en ce moys bertu r.e force abonde
Non plus que quant sij ans a bng enfant.

11 BOOK OF HOURS FOR THE USE OF ROME

Bellemare group (Rosenwald Master), *Job on the Dungheap*
France, 1524
Ink, paint, and gold on parchment, 23.3 × 14.9 cm
Library of Congress, Washington, Rosenwald MS 14, fols. 79v–80r

This illumination, with the date 1524 in the upper portion of the frame, opens the office of the Dead in this book of hours. It appears to be the earliest of the manuscripts attributed to the Bellemare Group, and in terms of layout, figure style, and colors, it closely resembles the hours of Jean II de Mauléon (no. 12). The figures' elegant costumes and postures, as well as the sweeping landscape backgrounds, are hallmarks of this group of illuminators. This manuscript shows influences from a number of prominent artists working in Italy as well as north of the Alps, but the closest comparisons are with contemporary paintings from Antwerp, and it is possible that some, or all, of the illuminators in the Bellemare group trained in Antwerp (see page 19). The gold frame around this miniature is common in many books of hours made by this group, but such borders, which draw on Italian sources, were popular in early sixteenth-century French illumination, and similar frames can be found in manuscripts made by other artisans and also in contemporary printed books (nos. 7, 8).

KBG

AD MATVTINVM PROFID
DELIBVS DEF
VNCTIS

Inuitatorium Regem cui omnia viuunt Ve
nite adoremus. Regem cui omnia &c.

VENITE Exultemus domino: iubile
mus deo salutari nostro: praeoccupe
mus faciem eius in confessione: et in psalmis iu
bilemus ei. Regem cui omnia viuunt: venite ado
remus. Quoniam deus magnus dominus
et rex magnus super omnes deos: quoniam non
repellet dominus plebem suam: quia in manu
eius sunt omnes fines terrae: et altitudines mon
tium ipse conspicit. Venite adoremus.
Quoniam ipsius est mare: et ipse fecit illud
et aridam fundauerunt manus eius: venite ado
remus et procidamus ante deum: ploremus co
ram domino qui fecit nos: quia ipse est domi
nus deus noster: nos autem populus eius: et o
ues pascuae eius. Regem cui omnia viuunt: ve
nite adoremus. Hodie si vocem eius audieri
tis: nolite obdurare corda vestra: sicut in exacer
batione secundum diem tentationis in deserto

12 BOOK OF HOURS FOR THE USE OF TOULOUSE

Bellemare group (Master of Jean II de Mauléon), *Bathsheba*
France (Tours?), c. 1523
Ink, paint, and gold on parchment, 17.7 × 10.8
Walters Art Museum, MS w.449, fol. 76r

This book was made for Jean II de Mauléon, probably to mark his con-
firmation as bishop of the Augustinian foundation of Saint-Bertrand at
Comminges. The Seven Penitential Psalms were a standard textual compo-
nent of books of hours. This text is sometimes opened with a scene of David
in prayer, or, as in this case, the reason for David's penance. Here Bathsheba,
at her bath, receives a message from David, who is visible in the tower in
the background. David's request that Bathsheba come to him will result in
his adultery with her, eventually causing him much difficulty. The selection
of this particular scene for a bishop's personal devotional book is puzzling,
especially given the high degree of sensuality in the depiction of the nude
Bathsheba, and the shell of Venus (a clearly secular reference) in the frame.
The page facing this one includes de Mauléon's motto, *Omnis Amor Tecum*
(all of my love is with you). The motto was certainly intended to refer to a
love of God, but the proximity of the motto to a depiction of a naked woman
allows for a more profane interpretation. Perhaps an interest in contemporary
artistic trends was more important to the patron than the subject matter: the
Bathsheba and other illuminations in this book show similarities to the work
of several prominent contemporary artists, including Albrecht Dürer. Scenes
like this one, with secular undertones, are found in manuscripts produced for
other patrons by the Bellemare group.

KBG

13 BOOK OF HOURS FOR THE USE OF ROME

Bellemare group (Doheny Master?), *Saint John the Evangelist Receiving the Revelation*
France (Tours?), c. 1525
Ink, paint, and gold on parchment, 8.9 × 5.4
Private collection, Washington, fol. iv

This manuscript is unique in that all of the pictures are completely devoid of human figures. The artist does not depict the scenes traditionally associated with each of the texts in the book, but instead shows only the backgrounds of those scenes, like empty stages with no actors. At the start of the Gospel lessons one would expect to find a scene of John the Evangelist on Patmos, experiencing the vision described in the Book of Revelation. In this miniature only the setting is shown, with John's book and pen case scattered on the ground, and the hand of God with an open book extending from the heavens, but without John himself. The purpose of this might be to encourage the viewer to imagine the figures into the scene, and perhaps to place him or herself in the midst of the event depicted. This scene is modeled on the scene of John devouring the book in Albrecht Dürer's widely known *Apocalypse* series of woodcuts (1498). On the evidence of its creative approach to traditional iconography and an association with the Bellemare group, this manuscript has been tentatively attributed to the patronage of Jean Lallemant the Younger († 1548). It does not, however, display the emblematic, visionary, and highly personal imagery of the other books associated with Lallemant, and neither his name nor his arms appear, so the connection remains highly speculative. The book was likely a rectangle when it was first made; the present shape is the result of heavy trimming by a later owner, perhaps to remove damaged portions or to fit it to this particular binding. As can be seen in this example, parts of the rectangular frames surrounding the miniatures throughout the book were cut off by this trimming.

KBG

14 BOOK OF HOURS FOR THE USE OF BOURGES

Attributed to Bellemare group, *Device of Jean Lallemant the Younger*
France (Bourges?), 1506
Ink, paint, and gold on parchment, 13.6 × 7.6 cm
Library of Congress, Washington, Rosenwald MS 12, fols. 14v–15r

All of the books of hours made for Jean Lallemant the Younger († 1548) share common features, but this example is particularly close to MS w.446 (no. 15). Lallemant and other members of his family seem to have been interested in emblems and other symbolic motifs with personal significance. The Gospel lessons open with a full-page miniature of Jean Lallemant's device: a red lion, holding in his mouth a plumed helmet from which the Lallemant arms are suspended. The lion holds a blue book above his head—the book with seven seals described in the Book of Revelation—inscribed with the motto *delear prius* (I shall perish first). The same book appears in the small miniature on the facing page, and is found throughout this and other books of hours associated with Jean Lallemant the Younger. The curtain behind the lion is strewn with gold letters. These do not form words or a recognizable anagram, but Lilian Randall (*Medieval and Renaissance Manuscripts in the Walters Art Gallery* [Baltimore and London, 1992], vol. 2, part 2, 540) has deduced that they correspond to a table found in this book and can be deciphered to give the date of the manuscript. The small, framed miniature on folio 15r is one of forty similar pictures throughout this manuscript, each with the same background, and the same series of gold letters. The subject matter of these miniatures alternates between the sealed book and a hair shirt, indicating penitence. The book can be associated with John the Evangelist, author of the Book of Revelation, and the hair shirt with John the Baptist. As several members of the Lallemant family were named Jean, the family seems to have had a special interest in these saints.

KBG

Initium sancti euangelii secū
dum Ioannem. Gloria tibi domi
ne.

IN prin
cipio e
rat verbum et
verbum erat a
pud deum, et
deus erat ver
bum. Hoc erat in principio apud
deum. Omnia per ipsum facta
sunt: et sine ipso factum est ni
hil quod factum est. In ipso vi
ta erat, et vita erat lux hominū
et lux in tenebris lucet, et tene
bræ eam non comprehenderat
Fuit homo missus a deo cui no
men erat Ioannes. Hic venit in
testimonium vt testimonium
perhiberet de lumine, vt omnes
crederent per illum. Non erat ille
lux, sed vt testimonium perhibe

15 BOOK OF HOURS FOR THE USE OF ROME

Attributed to Bellemare group,
Hair Shirt and Flight into Egypt
France (Tours?), c. 1524
Ink, paint, and gold on parchment, 15.7 × 9.7
Walters Art Museum, MS w.446, fol. 37v

Of the manuscripts believed to have been owned by Jean Lallemant the Younger (†1548), this is the only one that does not include his coat of arms or other clear indications of a connection with him. The striking similarity between the imagery in this book and that in the Rosenwald collection (no. 14), however, strongly suggests that Jean was indeed the patron. This is further supported by the use of similar emblems and other motifs in several properties owned by the Lallemant family and renovated under his supervision. The miniatures in this book alternate between a blue seraph holding a closed book inscribed *delear prius* (I shall perish first), and a hair shirt visible behind a torn curtain. In each picture, a small devotional scene is visible just above the emblem: for example, on this page the Flight into Egypt is depicted just above the hair shirt. The hair shirt is related to John the Baptist, a namesake of several members of the Lallemant family, and also to penitence and humility. These were likely in the mind of Jean, who, at the time this book was commissioned, was living under the accusation of financial fraud. This book may have served as an updated version of the book of hours in the Rosenwald collection (no. 14), with which it shares many features. The Baltimore manuscript, however, has several indications of a strong interest in the Franciscan order, which, owing to the patronage of Anne de Bretagne (1477–1514), had become increasingly popular with the French nobility.

KBG

16 BOOK OF HOURS FOR THE USE OF ROME

Attributed to Bellemare group, *Tower of Tribulation* and *Crucifixion*
France (Tours?), c. 1535
Ink, paint, and gold on parchment, 18.9 × 12.9
Walters Art Museum, MS W.451, fol. 76v

This book of hours was made for Jean Lallemant the Younger († 1548), who was imprisoned for fraud from 1535 to 1537. Lallemant wrote an inscription on the flyleaf with the date 1536, so he must have had this book with him while he was in prison. The emblematic imagery is typical of books made for Jean: individual elements of the picture can be interpreted in several ways, as parts of a riddle with personal significance. Earlier books of hours made for Lallemant included the emblem of the hair shirt, indicating a strong interest in penitence and humility. Here, the hair shirt is not an abstract emblem, but is worn by a figure imprisoned in a tower. This figure has been understood to be Lallemant himself, in the guise of John the Baptist, praying for his release. John the Baptist was a namesake of Jean and several members of his family, and Jean seems to have identified closely with him, perhaps because both were unjustly accused and imprisoned. In each of the seven towers illustrated in this manuscript (seven also being the number of penitential psalms), the prisoner raises his hands in prayer and looks toward a small, devotional image in the heavens, in this case the Crucifixion. Each of the towers is labeled *tribulatio* (tribulation), with the words *spes* (hope) at the base and *patientia* (patience) at the top, encouraging Lallemant to endure his present difficulties. In several early sixteenth-century treatises associated with François Desmoulins, towers represented virtue, and Geoffroy Tory (c. 1480–1533) associated them with Bourges. The locked chest forming the base of the tower, inscribed with the word *spes*, could refer to Pandora's box. The calendar of this manuscript has been attributed to Jean Pichore.

KBG

17 HYPNEROTOMACHIA POLIPHILI

Franciscus Columna (1433?–1527), *The Second Triumph*
Printed by Aldus Manutius, Venice 1499
Woodcut on paper, 30 × 25 cm
Private collection, Washington, fols. Kvii—Kviii

The *Hypnerotomachia Poliphili* (Poliphilo's struggle for love in a dream) is as dense and obscure as its title suggests. It narrates the adventures of the lovers Poliphilo and Polia, as Poliphilo experienced them in a dream. During the dream Poliphilo searches for Polia, finds her, and declares his love for her. Together they proceed to a temple to become engaged. Along the way they encounter five different triumphal processions, celebrating the union of lovers. The second procession, or triumph, is that of the nymph Leda and Zeus, in the guise of a swan. The illustration, displayed across two pages, is packed with symbolic references, from the sarcophagus-shaped cart to the shapes and types of standards. The woodcut complicates rather than simplifies the understanding of the text, written in a unique mixture of Latin and Italian regional dialects. For all its complexity, the *Hypnerotomachia* shakes loose the bonds between text and image that had governed medieval book illustration. The novelty of its concept as well as the beauty of the typography declared the success of the Manutius edition, which soon became one of the most influential books of the Renaissance.

MB

Sopra de questo superbo & Triumphale uectabulo, uidi uno bianchissimo Cycno, negli amorosi amplexi duna inclyta Nympha filiola de Theseo, dincredibile bellecia formata, & cum el diuino rostro obsculantise, demisse le ale, tegeua le parte denudate della igenua Hera, Et cū diuini & uoluptici oblectamenti istauano delectabilmente iucundissimi ambi connexi, Et el diuino Olore tra le delicate & niuee coxe collocato. Laquale commodamente sedeua sopra dui Puluini di panno doro, exquisitamente di mosticula lanugine tomentati, cum tutti gli sumptuosi & ornanti correlarii opportuni. Et ella induta de uesta Nympha le subtile, de serico bianchissimo cum trama doro texto præluccente Agli loci competenti elegante ornato de petre pretiose.

Sencia defecto de qualunque cosa che ad incremento di dilecto uenustamente concorre. Summamente agli intuenti conspicuo & delectabile. Cum tutte le parte che

al primo fue descripto

di laude & plau

so.

*

EL TERTIO cæleste triumpho seguiua cum quatro uertibile rote di Chrysolitho æthiopico scintule doro flammigiante, Traiecta per elquale la seta del Asello gli maligni dæmonii fuga, Alla leua mano grato, cum tutto quello cõ di sopra di rote e dicto. Dapo scia le assule sue in ambito per el modo compacte sopra narrato, erano di uirente Helitropia Cyprico, cum potere negli lumi cælesti, el suo gestate cœla, & il diuinare dona, di sanguine guttule punctulato.

Offeriua tale historiato in sculpto la tabella dextra. Vno homo di regia maiestate isigne, Oraua in uno sacro templo el diuo simulacro, quel lo che della formosissima fiola deueua seguire. Sentendo el patre la eiectione sua per ella del regno. Et ne per alcuno fusse pregna, Fece una munita structura di una excelsa torre, Et in quella cum soléne custodia la fece inclaustrare. Nella quale ella cessabonda assedédo, cum excessiuo solatio, nel uirgi

neo sino gutte do

ro stillare

uede

ua.

*

In 1529, after a trip to Italy, where he met the influential Venetian printer Aldus Manutius, Geoffroy Tory published his *Champ fleury*, a treatise on typography aimed at introducing the latest currents of Italian humanism to France. In this opening, the letter *Y* becomes the symbol of the choices facing Hercules at the crossroads: one branch leads to virtue and the other to vice. At the left, easy steps lead a man to an orgy of food and his inevitable fall into the fires of hell, while on the right, a difficult course under attack from Superbia (pride), Invidia (envy), and Libido (lust) takes the climber to Wisdom. An intellectual deeply engaged in the rebirth of French letters, Tory was born in Bourges and later settled in Paris, where he published editions of the classics. Tory's manual is influenced by Franciscus Columna's *Hypnerotomachia Poliphili* (no. 17), which, with its enigmatic pictures and complex rhetorical strategies, contributed greatly to a new understanding of the relationship between words and images in illustrated texts. Tory's moralizations are still very much informed by medieval pictorial strategies: the mountains of sausages to indicate luxury, and the climb up a ladder to reach wisdom, are common symbols in medieval art. By demonstrating the poten-

Inuidia,

Superbia,

Libido,

I En porrois dire beaucop daultres belles cho=
ses, mais pour ceste heure ie passeray oul=
tre, venant a deseigner & descrire
nostre derniere lettre Abecedai
re & Attique Zeta. Laquel
le Frere Lucas Paciolus
na pas mise en sa Di
uina proportione,
et la cause pour=
quoy il a omi=
se, ie ne le pu
is entedre,
ne ne me
soucye.

Frere Lu
cas Pa=
ciolus,

19 BOOK OF HOURS

Geoffroy Tory (c. 1480–1533), *Annunciation*
Printed by Olivier Mallard, Paris, 1542
Woodcut on paper, 15.1 × 10 cm
Library of Congress, Washington, Rosenwald 1020, fols. Dii–Diii

Tory started printing books of hours in 1525, when he first introduced his minimalist designs as an alternative to the hackneyed productions of contemporary French printers: the illustrations in printed French books of hours had been stifled by routine reproductions of old models and the obsessive repetition of decorative motifs like the *criblé* backgrounds and heavy architectural frames. In comparison, Tory's designs move gracefully over the white page, as the outlines of the figures dance in spacious compositions. The roots of Tory's new style are to be sought in his knowledge of Italian book illuminations and in particular of the achievements introduced by the *Hypnerotomachia Poliphili* (no. 17). In this 1452 edition printed by Mallard (active 1535–1544), the full-page illustrations derive from the cuts that Tory had designed for his 1529 miniature (16mo) edition, while the borders are composed of those he had used for his 1527 edition. The latter were based on designs first published by Jean du Pre (active 1514–1526) in the 1490s and were still greatly indebted to the late medieval manuscript botanical tradition. Tory's ability lies in adjusting the dynamism and elegance of the Italian Renaissance woodcut to the manuscript tradition of French *horae*. His designs proved to be extremely influential in the development of French woodcut design. The coat-of-arms and the capital *F* at the bottom of both pages refer to King François I, who had appointed Tory *imprimeur du roi* (printer to the king) in 1531.

MB

Omꝑe labea mea
aperies.
tos meũ annũ
eiabit laudẽ tuã.

eus in adiutorium meum
intende.
omine ad adiuuandũ me
festina.

20 COMPILATION OF RHYMED PROVERBS

Proverb
France (Savoy), c. 1490
Ink on parchment, 20.5 × 13.6
Walters Art Museum, MS W.313, fol. 17r

This book contains 182 proverbs in rhyming French verse. Compiled from a variety of sources, they relate to a wide range of situations and include some ideas familiar to us today, such as "don't look a gift horse in the mouth." Each proverb is illustrated with a single drawing, usually monochrome, that is a literal interpretation of the words. In order to understand the picture a reader must already be familiar with the proverb. The book, written and illustrated with brown ink on paper, appears to have been made for the bourgeois market rather than for an upper-class patron, and it was likely meant to be amusing rather than morally instructive. Several similar books of rhyming proverbs have survived, but they are rare; it is unclear whether the low survival rate is a result of the books being well used and therefore quickly worn out, or owing to a limited production in the first place. This book appears to be incomplete, and there is evidence that it has been misbound, perhaps during a repair.

KBG

Probé

Son bon pñre bug don
De franche voulente
Soit de value ou non
Il doit estre accepte
Sant estre ambonne
Ne short ne dedens
Car a cheual donne
Ne regarde les dens

21 BOOK OF HOURS FOR THE USE OF ROME

Rebus
Printed by Germain Hardouyn, Paris, 1524
Woodblock on parchment, 15.2 × 7.5 cm
Walters Art Museum, 92.82, fol. N

In the mid-1520s Germain Hardouyn began to publish books of hours in an elongated format similar to that which Aldus Manutius (1449–1515) had used for his popular editions of the classics. However, to enhance the similarities with manuscript books, in this edition printed on parchment, the illustrations are framed by *all'antica* borders that are painted and not printed. In addition, the prints are colored in with a thick layer of paint that masks the outlines. It was quite common at this time to place a rebus such as this one at the end of books of hours. In this case the solution to the rebus is given underneath the picture for each word. This is an indication that the word puzzle was used as mnemonic tool to learn a prayer or even a sequence of prayers dedicated to the Virgin. In fact, each line repeats a common attribute of the Virgin, for example, the Gate of Heaven and the Tower of David.

MB

Porte du ciel

Dame de preexcellence

Trompe a cor dant

Qui dez riglez raz pelle

Tour de Dauid

Aux mons dains asseurance

Port de salut

Cler mirouer a pu celle.

22 RATIONARUM EVANGELISTARUM

Figure for the Gospel of John
Printed by Thomas Anselm, Pforzheim (Germany), 1510
Woodcut on paper, 20.5 × 14 cm
Walters Art Museum, 92.394, fol. Aiii r

Between 1423 and 1426 Petrus von Rosenheim (1380–1433) composed his *Roseum Memoriale Divinorum Eloquiorum*, a poem of 1,194 distychs that summarized the content of all the books in the Bible, with the aim of facilitating its memorization. The *Rationarum Evangelistarum*, a pictoral guide to remembering the Gospels, derives from this earlier text and was published by Thomas Anselm in 1502. Anselm used the picture cycle that had appeared in the block-book *Ars Memorandi per Figuras Evangelistarum*, an anonymous mnemonic manual printed for the first time in 1470. Anselm's edition had an immediate popular appeal and was reprinted in 1507 and 1510. Each Gospel is summarized by three or four composite pictures. Every image is constructed around the symbol of one Evangelist, to which smaller pictures symbolizing different passages of his Gospel have been added. In the first of the four figures dedicated to the Gospel of John, the eagle (his symbol) is strung with various objects that refer to the first six chapters of his Gospel. The pair of heads and the dove that spring from the eagle's head signify the Trinity and indicate the beginning of the Gospel of John. The lute at the center stands for banquet music and for the wedding at Cana, the wound for the chapter on Nicodemus, the bucket for the Samaritan woman, the fish at the left for the probatic pool, and the fishes and loaves with the Eucharistic host at the right relate to the miracle of the feeding of the five thousand. Each attribute has a number, keyed to a list of chapters on the opposing verso. Poetic dystichs, beginning with progressive letters of the alphabet for easy recall, further explain the attributes.

MB

23 ICONES HISTORIARUM VETERIS TESTAMENTI

Hans Holbein the Younger (1497–1543), *Psalm 52*
Printed by Jean Frellon, Lyon, 1547
Woodcut on paper, 19 × 13.5 cm
Walters Art Museum, 92.239, fol. Kiii v

Each page of the *Icones Historiarum Veteris Testamenti* (Picture of the Stories of the Old Testament) is dedicated to one of the books of the Old Testament. At the top of each page, a passage in Latin condenses the biblical chapter and serves as the title for the woodcut below. At the bottom, French verses explain the biblical reference and situate it in the narrative context of the Bible. Hans Holbein designed the series of pictures for this figurative Bible and chose the traditional image of the fool to illustrate Psalm 52. In the woodcut, the children surrounding the main figure are presumably the children of men mentioned in the text of the psalm (verse 3), but their relationship with the fool is unclear, and no explanation is offered in the French text below. The ambiguity of the image offers the reader the possibility of discursive explanation. Gilles Corrozet (1510–1568), a humanist publisher and author of a collection of emblems, wrote the French text. In his introduction to the book, Corrozet urges readers to use the plates to decorate their houses so that by frequently gazing upon the biblical stories, they would carve the sacred stories in their minds. The value of ambiguous images to enhance mnemonic recollection was a recourse of emblematic literature as well. The edition of the *Icones Historiarum* published by Jean Frellon (active 1508–1528), was the fourth edition of the original cuts and the second edition of the text in Latin and French.

MB

PSALTES contra Iudæos excãdescit, ac eos
qui CHRISTVM Messiam Deum in lege
promissum infideliter, & impiè abnegant,
insipientes vocat.

PSALM LII.

Folz sont ceux là (come escrit le Psalmiste)
Qui en leurs cueurs dient que Iesus Christ
N'est Messias, Dauid tant s'en contriste,
Qu'en plusieurs lieux encontre iceux escrit.

24 BOOK OF EMBLEMS

Andrea Alciati (1492–1550), *Princes*
Printed by Matthias Bonhomme for Guillaume Rouille, Lyon, 1548
Woodcut on paper, 19 × 13 cm
Walters Art Museum, 92.24, fol. Hii

Simply described, emblems are a combination of a title, a picture, and a poetic explanation shaped around a word rich in meaning. Andrea Alciati, an Italian jurist and intellectual, wrote the first collection of emblems, which he published in 1531. The Rouille Bonhomme editions of Alciati became very popular and were reprinted more than thirty-five times. Their success was due in part to the beautiful woodcuts framed by rich borders, designed by P. Vase (Pierre Eskrich) (1530–1590). In the book of emblems, an anchor with a dolphin wrapped around its shaft represents the idea of leadership. The motto above reads, "the prince ensures the safety of his subjects." The poem below explains the association of the title and the picture: when sailors throw the anchor overboard in order to stabilize the ship, dolphins wrap around the anchor to keep it steady. Therefore, the explanation continues, princes should use this image because they are to the people what the anchor is to sailors. In the works of a number of classical authors, the anchor was a common symbol of political steadfastness. The dolphin and anchor combination, however, would have been better known as a picture of Emperor Vespasian's motto *festina lente* (make haste slowly), where the speed of the dolphin was seen to temper the weight of the anchor. The ambiguity of the picture is typical of emblematic literature, which exploited images for their mnemonic and interpretive potential.

MB

PRINCEPS.

Princeps subditorum incolumitatem procurans.

Titanij quoties conturbant æquora fratres,
  Tum miseros nautas anchora iacta iuuat.
Hanc pius erga homines Delphin complectitur: imis
  Tutius ut possit figier illa uadis.
Quàm decet hæc memores gestare insignia Reges?
  Anchora quod nautis, se populo esse suo?

Photography credits: Albertina, Vienna: p. 18; Bibliothèque nationale de France: p. 24; The Hague, Koninklijke Bibliotheek: p. 22; Library of Congress: pp. 61, 67, 77; Bernard Pobiak, Pubcomm Group, NY: pp. 19, 39, 41, 44–47, 50–59, 63–65, 68–75, 79–87; Réunion des Musées Nationaux /Art Resource, NY: p. 16; Susan Tobin, The Walters Art Museum: pp. 42–43; V&A Images/Victoria & Albert Museum: p. 21

Edited by Mary Yakush

Design by Jennifer A. Corr
Typeset in Adobe Jenson Pro and Charlemagne Std

Printed by Finlay, Bloomfield, Connecticut, on 100# Utopia One Matte Text